CULTURAL AFFAIRS AND
FOREIGN RELATIONS

 The American Assembly, *Columbia University*

917.3 aa

CULTURAL AFFAIRS AND FOREIGN RELATIONS

Prentice-Hall, Inc., *Englewood Cliffs, N.J.*
A SPECTRUM BOOK

43725-

Preface

The essays presented herewith were prepared as background material for participants in the Twenty-second American Assembly, *Cultural Affairs and Foreign Relations,* at Arden House, the Harriman Campus of Columbia University, October 18-21, 1962, and for subsequent international, regional, and local Assemblies as well as for the general reader.

Edited by Robert Blum, the papers discuss the connections between United States activities overseas in education, science and the arts, and the conduct of international relations.

As a nonpartisan, educational institution, The American Assembly neither endorses nor takes a stand on the views expressed in this volume. Nor are The Hazen Foundation and The Danforth Foundation, whose generosity has made this Assembly program possible, to be associated with recommendations growing out of it.

Henry M. Wriston
Chairman
The American Assembly

Table of Contents

Robert Blum, Editor

Introduction:

The Flow of People and Ideas

International cultural relations are as old as the flow of people and ideas across national boundaries. Recently, however, they have gained new dimensions as a result of the increased volume and growing complexity of international exchanges and contacts, the innovations of science and improved communications, the preoccupations of the cold war, the addition of many new states to the international community, and the multiplication of governmental activity. What we see today has, therefore, little resemblance to the traditional pattern of earlier periods.

The subject is not one that is sharply defined, and events are constantly overtaking attempts at neat classification. There is properly more concern with the purposes, methods and achievements of a rather loosely defined and rapidly developing area of activities than with a precise analysis of its nature. Neither the evolutionary *Kultur* of the German tradition, nor the refined arts and letters of French *culture,* nor the all embracing "culture" of the modern sociologists and anthropologists adequately characterizes the object of our concern, which is to some extent all of these, although none really fits.

Before his recent appointment as director of China Policy Studies at the Council on Foreign Relations, Robert Blum was for nine years President of The Asia Foundation. He is a trustee of the Carnegie Endowment for International Peace and was from 1956 to 1962 a member of the United States National Commission for UNESCO. Dr. Blum was an assistant to the Secretary of Defense from 1947 to 1949 and then served with the foreign aid program in Europe and Asia, where in 1950-51 he was head of the economic aid mission to Indo-China. In 1953 Dr. Blum was staff director of the President's Committee on International Information and Related Activities.

1

The dynamism of cultural relations

In general we are interested in the exchange of ideas and cultural values among nations. This takes place in innumerable ways and at countless points of contact. More particularly, our interest is in the more effective encouragement and management of this exchange. Yet, the cultural influences at work between nations have a dynamism that is far more compelling than the planned "cultural relations" and "cultural exchanges" for which the professional persons in the field have a special responsibility. The activities that they guide do not exclusively or even most importantly set the tone for the most significant exchanges of ideas and cultural values. The spread of political ideologies propelled by national power, the urge for economic development, the international exchange of equipment and goods, as well as the tourist, the business man, the soldier, and news reporter—all provide vitality and substance to international cultural relations.

Even though we need to make our subject manageable in terms of what government and private organizations have done and should do, we must not lose sight of the total, complex pattern of international cultural exchange, nor limit our understanding simply because we have to narrow our focus. Against the historical and current background of United States interest in international cultural affairs, our concern in this book will be principally with education, science, and the arts and humanities. Although we write of programs and organizations, educational exchanges and libraries, conferences and art exhibits, these represent only a small part of the streams of cultural influence that flow within the international community. This is particularly true at a time of social and political upheavals such as the present, when traditional patterns are upset, ideologies clash, and communications are rapid, voluminous, complex and often strident.

To these upheavals, the United States and the Western world have contributed mightily with their ideals of political and social democracy and economic doctrines of industrialization and mass consumption. Peoples have been stirred, ambitions fired, and nations created from these movements, which have not readily found constructive substitutes for the traditions that have been corroded. It is surely an obligation for us to do what we can so as to exercise our cultural influence in a helpful way and not be content to allow the doctrines of the West to provide nothing more than the inspiration for uncontrolled change. This is essentially a cultural task, requiring a clear conception of our own values and of the way in which we want to share them with others.

What George N. Shuster, in the first chapter, calls the "international dimension" has become an inextricable part of our lives. It is not merely in the more obvious realms of politics, military strategy, and economics that this is so, but "in the minds of men," to quote from the charter of UNESCO. The diffusion of scientific knowledge, the interdependence of nations, and the inter-penetration of the ambitions and frustrations of the peoples of the world mean that the exchanges of ideas, of learning, and of information are of major importance to modern man. This is especially true for a society such as that of the United States which prides itself on being an "open society," and which aspires to be in the vanguard of progress, reflecting in its ideals the hopes of mankind. These objectives cannot be achieved with a mind that is closed to the thoughts or ungenerous to the needs of others. Cultural activities, therefore, must not be thought of merely as a means of bringing foreign students to this country and sending American books and professors abroad, with the general purpose of helping others. They are also a way for us to understand others better, and, in seeing ourselves as others see us, we may understand ourselves better and clarify our own role in the world. This is the meaning of the "two way street," which is more a state of mind than a highway, and which we have to honor with more than lip service.

This suggests the necessity of thinking of cultural activities not merely as an adjunct of our foreign aid program or of our international information and propaganda activities. These are of great importance, to be sure, but it would be a misunderstanding of the cultural field to regard it simply as a means of expressing and extending American political influence. W. McNeil Lowry and Gertrude S. Hooker stress, in their chapter on the arts and humanities, the importance of respecting the integrity of cultural activities and of not impairing the vitality and needs of the artists themselves. Roger Revelle, who writes of the "two faces of science," points to the dilemma of reconciling political considerations with the free quest of the individual for truth, and sees a similarity between the position of the artist and that of the scientist. How to give international cultural activities the encouragement they require without impairing the essential freedom of the artist, scientist, scholar, and critic is a challenge to the very conception of a free society. If, to receive the support, the price in terms of control and manipulation is high, it would be better not to pay it, for we would be undermining the very principles we espouse.

Cultural activities and national policy

An understanding of the cultural and social environment in which we have to carry out our national policies is indispensable to the effectiveness of those policies. Moreover, that environment is one of the elements we have to influence in order to make our policies effective. In a very real sense, therefore, the cultural dimension does not consist of expendable frills, but is an essential ingredient of national activity. So far, our words recognizing this have not always been followed by deeds, and an adequate concern for the cultural ingredient in national policy has yet to be translated into an effective demonstration that its importance is in fact recognized. At the governmental level, only the Congress, the President and the Secretary of State can accomplish this, and abroad the cultural affairs officer can do little without the leadership and support of his Ambassador. This requires not merely the Ambassador's approval of a variety of activities labeled "culture," but the active involvement of cultural considerations in the day-to-day conduct of the Embassy's business. Foreign policy cannot be effective without it. To paraphrase Clemenceau: cultural relations are too important to be left to the cultural affairs officer.

The vast foreign aid and substantial information programs of the United States government have, all too often, suffered from an inadequate appreciation of the cultural environment in which they operate and a failure to weigh the cultural and social—not to say political—consequences of these activities. As a result, they have often lacked effectiveness or have had results different from what was planned or anticipated. The United States, with its far-flung influence and activities throughout the world, is under a special obligation to understand the environment in which it is working and the effect its actions have on the cultural traditions and social attitudes of others.

Moreover, cultural activities themselves have often suffered from the disdain of being regarded as nice but inconsequential, or from the unreasonable expectation that they are capable of solving immediate political problems. The critics have often tried to have it both ways by treating cultural activities with disdain and then laying such a heavy burden of responsibility on them as to make the contempt that follows failure an easy game. Activities which should have their sole justification in their own aesthetic, educational, or humanistic qualities are too often expected to achieve results that are unrealistic, or blamed for not achieving results the responsibility for which lies elsewhere. This results from the frequent failure to distinguish between the different purposes that cultural activities are intended to serve, or capable of serving. An incorrect analysis of situations is the result, and, all too often, leads either to naive prescriptions for complicated matters, or recriminations because of the inability of cultural activities to solve problems or prevent unfavorable situations which are in fact due to other causes. Conversely, because of the substantial universality of many forms of scientific, artistic and intellectual pursuits, cultural activities may be under suspicion for fear of their undermining rigidly held political attitudes.

These misunderstandings are a price we pay for living in a highly charged political atmosphere in which the political test—and often a short-range one at that—pervades almost all forms of international discourse. In this respect, the cultural field is no different from the scientific and others, which enjoy the lavish bounty of political attention while feeling the restraints and pressures imposed by politics. It would be unrealistic to expect that cultural activities can be divorced from political considerations, especially when government is so deeply involved in these matters, but there is surely a wise and necessary distinction to be made between short-sighted and self-defeating attempts at political and propagandistic manipulation on the one hand, and, on the other, the encouragement and support of cultural activities as an enlightened expression of national policy and a reflection of our national character. The pressures of the cold war make it difficult to formulate these distinctions and even more difficult to apply them.

In a democratic society like the United States the delineation of government's role in these affairs is a sensitive and difficult matter. The diversity within a democratic society does not permit the government to command the nation's cultural life. The communist countries have no such difficulty in reconciling their cultural tradition with their political purposes or in devising international policies and procedures consistent with what is done domestically. The church's missionary work, one of the best established expressions of international cultural activity, has not had to contend with this dilemma, either. In America, the decentralized and highly diversified structure of educational and cultural life creates for the government the further problem of how most effectively to tap the resources—the artists, teachers, scientists and books—that are needed for international cultural activities, but that are not normally subject to government control.

This situation gives to non-governmental participation its special importance in United States cultural activities abroad. This participation reflects the tradition of diversified non-governmental support of these activities, the inability of government to speak fully for the nation in such matters, and the ability of non-governmental bodies to perform, in some respects, more effectively than government. This situation creates, however, a need for some form of consultation or even coordination between private and governmental endeavors and between private activities and governmental policy. The question also arises whether new institutions and techniques need to be developed which will effectively reconcile the diverse resources and considerations, both government and private, at work in American society so that they are most expressive internationally of the humanistic values as well as the political purposes of the country.

These values and purposes need to be compatible in the long run, although their confrontation often creates difficulties in individual cases. The following chapters reveal a constant awareness of the interrelationship between cultural activities and national policy. Yet, both explicitly and tacitly, they see for international cultural relations a role and an importance that are not limited by current political preoccupations. For example, cultural exchanges between the United States and the communist countries receive attention as do the international cultural activities of the communist countries. However, what the United States is doing, and should do, is not seen by any of the authors as merely a response to what the communists are doing. This is a political consideration that cannot be ignored, but to place it at the center of our attention would be to misunderstand the true long-term significance of international cultural activities, to be drawn toward a policy of imitation and response rather than self-reliant initiative and to place on cultural activities an unrealistic responsibility for achieving immediate political results.

In recent years, new impetus has been given to cultural activities as an important part of foreign aid programs, particularly in the newly developing parts of the world. The training of foreign students and the establishment of schools, libraries, laboratories and universities have become practical ways of contributing to the growth of new countries while imparting to them something of our cultural values. This new development, the antecedents of which are to be found in the colonial period, is dealt with particularly in Howard E. Wilson's chapter on education, a field where there has been a heavy flow of material and advisory assistance. The enthusiasm for these activities should not, however, obscure the view of international cultural relations as an expression of humanistic aspirations through the free flow of people and ideas. Nor should the emphasis on aid to less developed areas mislead us into thinking of cultural relations only in terms of those who help and those who are helped and into overlooking that we must receive and learn as well as give and teach.

W. McNeil Lowry and Gertrude S. Hooker urge that we not sacrifice our cultural ties with Europe to our newly found interest in Asia and Africa. As beneficiaries of European culture, it would be not only unwise, but a distortion of our own history. Moreover, it is in relation to Europe, whence we have learned so much, that we can best measure our own cultural achievements and test the reputation that our culture enjoys abroad. Our international cultural efforts are nourished by the character and quality of our cultural life at home. We cannot starve our operas, while feasting on comic books and television thrillers, and expect that by some magic the "image" of America can be made to look different from reality. The image abroad reflects the substance at home.

The task ahead

The following chapters reveal an astonishing variety of activities already undertaken and point to a diversity of tasks that will test our ingenuity, and, more importantly, the depth and quality of our own educational, scientific and artistic life. We are faced, in effect, by a new kind of international challenge that is not political in any narrow sense but requires that we compete in the market-place of ideas, talents and ideals. These are necessarily a reflection of our own society but should have something important to say to others. And, in addressing ourselves to others, it is not merely a small educated leadership that is our concern; but great numbers of people with whom we need to set up effective communication so that we understand their aspirations and they feel that we have something useful to convey to them. In a very real sense, therefore, the problems dealt with in this book affect deeply the position of the United States in the world and the ability of this country to maintain a position of leadership. As Philip H. Coombs writes in the final chapter, the task we face requires the best efforts of the government—which have not yet been forthcoming—together with the participation and vitality of the non-governmental organizations that help give our society its diversity and vigor.

George N. Shuster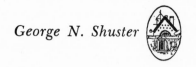

1

The Nature and Development
of United States Cultural Relations

Cultural relations in the modern sense have a relatively brief but impressive history. The major European colonizing powers, notably France, Germany and Great Britain, increasingly aware of their social responsibilities to the dependent peoples as well as of the reliance which necessarily had to be placed on native civil servants and ruling castes, came at the turn of the century to rely more and more on cultural influence as an instrumentality of cooperation. This experience was later made the basis of policy toward other nations. A remarkable network of services was developed, designed for all levels of education and often particularly concerned with the arts. The results achieved were frequently quite remarkable. Today we are seeing the extent to which all this has been merged with the cultures of the peoples once guided and influenced, but now independent.

THE ORIGINS

It was this development which furnished a spur and indeed a kind of model when during the administration of President Franklin D. Roosevelt

GEORGE N. SHUSTER, *president emeritus of Hunter College, is United States representative to the executive board of UNESCO and assistant to the president of Notre Dame University. He has been chairman of the Institute of International Education and a member of the general advisory committee to the Division of Cultural Relations in the State Department. Dr. Shuster has written numerous books on education, the latest being* The Ground I Walked On.

what has been familiarly termed the "Good Neighbor Policy" toward Latin America was inaugurated. To be sure, there had been some activity on the part of the United States in the area of cultural exchange prior to July 2, 1938, when a departmental order implementing the "Good Neighbor Policy" created the Division of Cultural Relations in the Department of State. Most of this activity had taken place as a result of private initiative, although the federal government had also been active in a modest way. The Smithsonian Institution had been authorized by the Congress to make provision for the export of literary and scientific materials. The indemnities accruing to this country as a result of the Boxer Rebellion were set aside by agreement with the government of China to assist students from that country. Upon occasion, ambassadors and consuls were to all intents and purposes cultural envoys as well.

But 1938 was a year of decision insofar as the public policy of the United States in the field of cultural relations is concerned. The subsequent stages in the formation and execution of that policy may be noted:

First, the pioneer efforts of the Division of Cultural Relations.

Second, the blending of cultural activities and propaganda during the war years and thereafter.

Third, the entry of the United States into the area of international cooperation, marked by the establishment of UNESCO in 1945 and 1946.

Fourth, subsequent efforts to insure a climate of mutuality and also to improve the quality of the operation.

We shall review these briefly (unfortunately there is no treatise which outlines them in desirable detail), so that the major issues can be discerned and some basis laid for projecting them into the future.

The Division of Cultural Relations

The Division of Cultural Relations was in many ways a novel undertaking. The staff of the State Department and a General Advisory Committee were conjoined in an effort to carry out, on behalf of the United States, the provisions of the Convention for the Promotion of Inter-American Cultural Activities, signed in Buenos Aires during 1937. Viewed in retrospect, this was a quite modest program, concerned primarily with the exchange of persons on a scale which now seems diminutive. It is, however, worthy of note that such exchanges would continue to remain of vital interest in every cultural relations program to follow. As time went on and war in Europe as well as in the Far East cast its tragic shadow on the world of man, China, Africa, and the Near East were included in the Division's concern. Later on, the Division also took under advisement the problem of how to assist German education in casting off the shackles of Nazism, and participated in planning for the future with the Conference of Ministers of Education in exile. But before much of this thinking could be transformed into some kind of practice the Department of State placed all its eggs in the propagandistic incubator of the Office of War Information.

In several respects, the Division of Cultural Relations established concepts which continue to be central in our thinking. First, the emphasis it placed on the exchange of persons has been retained, though the number of those involved is also incalculably greater. As a matter of fact, no one may actually know how many people are engaged, for in addition to such Exchange Programs as are sponsored by the Department of State and the Agency for International Development, there are those of the Armed Forces, the National Science Foundation, the Central Intelligence Agency, and other branches of the government.

Second, the Division threshed out in long and sometimes strenuous debates the question as to whether a cultural relations effort should be disinterested in character, or whether it ought frankly (or upon occasion covertly) to serve a propagandistic purpose. For obvious reasons, a program which relied solely on the mutual exchange of cultural achievement and experience came to seem impractical during the War and Cold War years. But, as we shall see, there has been a marked increase recently of support for the idea of having a body of cultural activities in which the national political interest is not directly involved.

Third, when in 1941 the Division established the post of Cultural Relations Officer (later on to be rechristened "Cultural Attaché"), the qualifications were these:

> . . . they should have a suitable personality that would assure their ability to work effectively with the people of the country in which they may be located; they should have broad intellectual and cultural interests, and should be capable of understanding and appreciating matters of which they may not have specialized knowledge; they should have constructive imagination and enthusiasm; their point of view should be that of a mature, educated person, and they should have good judgment and common sense. It may be assumed that they have a fluent command of the language of the country to which they are sent, but they should be willing to endeavor to learn to use the language with distinction as well as with readiness.

It is perhaps unnecessary to state that very few of our fellow citizens possessed the requirements thus outlined. The first time around some of them did, as witness Thornton Wilder, Charles Rufus Morey and Herschell Brickell. But the post was soon downgraded; the number of appointees was nevertheless legion, and some of the results were hair-raising. The United States was in certain instances represented by Cultural Relations Officers who should not have survived the sophomore year in any reputable college. Recently, however, the Department of State has thought of sending abroad at least a limited number of men and women whose qualifications would resemble those insisted upon in the days of yore by the Division of Cultural Relations.

Fourth, the General Advisory Committee, by reason of its interest in Latin America and the Near East in particular, promoted the idea of establishing American Libraries abroad and concerned itself directly with the then new Benjamin Franklin Library in Mexico City. It also began to consider ways in which American schools and colleges abroad, most of which had come into being on the initiative of missionary bodies, could be assisted by the government. The subsequent development of both these forms of endeavor is one of the major facts in the history of the cultural relations of the United States.

The influence of the British Council

But of all the reflections of the time described, no doubt those which had to do with the British Council continue to have the greatest influence, though no comparable institution was established in the United States. Those who are interested in the discussion of this very remarkable establishment may be referred to *The Cultural Approach,* by Ruth McMurray and Muna Lee. Here we shall merely note that the Council was a departure from normal British diplomatic practice. Though it had government financial support, it was nevertheless an organization of private citizens, many of whom had had years of experience abroad. The idea that the United States government could indirectly support private groups was at that time novel. But it has since become a quite normal procedure. In addition, the example of the British Council very greatly encouraged those who believed that an effective cultural relations program should be divorced from official propaganda.

Perhaps the most easily observable result of studying the activities of the British Council was that the Department of State began as early as 1939 to channel some of its cultural activities through private groups. The Institute of International Education started to serve as the operational agency for exchange grants, and the American Council of Education was active in the same field. Since that time, the number of such arrangements has greatly increased. Indeed, it may not be incorrect to say that one of the major innovations in the procedures of the federal government has been the transfer of operational responsibility for a number of its programs to private or semi-private groups and organizations.

This is the broad outline of the cultural relations policy of the United States until our entry into the Second World War. The titanic struggle was also much more a test of strength between conflicting ideologies than any previous war had been, save perhaps the initial stages of general

European resistance to the French Revolution. The British Council, as
a matter of fact, had come into being largely because it was thought
necessary to counteract the ruthless propaganda machine of Dr. Goebbels,
designed to till fields of the mind and the emotions in all parts of the
world. The cold war had begun, though probably no one realized it at
the time.

WAR TIME PROPAGANDA AND AFTERMATH

The Office of War Information into which the cultural program of the
Department of State was absorbed during the Second World War signaled
a relatively complete, though presumably temporary, victory for the point
of view that propaganda for the democratic philosophy of the United
States must always be the true purpose of cultural activities, however
discreetly camouflaged it might be. Indeed, this point of view remained
dominant in the Congress and elsewhere for a longer time than most observers had perhaps foreseen. It is therefore desirable to put it in some
sort of perspective.

The "American Century"

Wartime needs or the broader desirability of counteracting the vicious
though somehow, for many, attractive doctrines of the Nazis, were associated during the early forties with the belief, shared by a brilliant
group of historians, political theorists and publicists that the "American
Century" lay ahead. This would be a time in which the institutions and
basic "philosophy" of the United States would seem so self-evidently
right that all men who were capable of sound reason would desire them
for their countries. It was therefore imperative that the American people
realize their manifest destiny and set about, through a vigorous mission
of persuasion, to spread the gospel they had brought to fruition during
a century and a half. Here, then, was the obvious answer to the totalitar-
ians like Hitler. Another version of the American Century doctrine was
that of the "Anglo-Saxon heritage." For the advocates of this, British experience and American experience had fused in successfully making a
pragmatic demonstration of the superlative value of a free, constitution-
ally governed society.

Neither of these points of view was ever formally endorsed by the
United States government, but very competent writers expounded them
in pungent or eloquent prose. There was a good deal which could be said
in their favor. But perhaps it was not obvious enough then that if there
was to be an "American Century" the demand would have to come from
the peoples of the world rather than from our telling them that the

course of human destiny was in our hands. It would later on become clear that there was considerable reluctance around the globe to accepting the American Century with glee, especially when some of the salesmen neither knew what their wares were or how to make friends and influence people. Meanwhile the Congress tended to view the matter in the light of how much it was costing and how patriotic the merchandise could be deemed to be.

Office of War Information and successors

It is not within the scope of this essay to discuss the character or the achievements of the Office of War Information. What needs to be stressed, however, is that the OWI led to the creation of propagandistic instruments which would continue to be of great use, however perplexing it might on occasion be to decide on how to employ them. The most impressive of these are the United States Information Agency or Services, and of course the Voice of America.

Both are of importance to the development of our cultural relations policy, for a variety of reasons. The "American Century" idea was at first implicit in both. They were pressed into service after the war to insure the ideological renovation of Germany and Japan; and though there were marked differences between the methods used in the two countries, the basic common objective was to inculcate respect for, and if possible allegiance to, the democratic way of life. In what manner could this be more satisfactorily or effortlessly attained than through advertising the characteristics and achievements of the United States? The attempt necessarily required a good measure of experimentation, and it also became obvious that differences in social and political outlook would plague those in charge. The Voice of America was therefore often an object of praise, derision, or acceptance with a shrug of the shoulder. The Information Services fared somewhat better though they too sometimes found the going extremely difficult. A careful study of both (which of course cannot be attempted here) would undoubtedly provide a valuable commentary on the strength and the weakness of nationally sponsored propaganda activities.

The Voice of America was the first attempt made by the federal government to enter the highly important field of radio broadcasting. Several major problems presented themselves and have even now not been solved. First, the divorce between domestic broadcasting and government which is necessary under our laws and traditions made it impossible to carry over into propagandistic or information broadcasting abroad the experience and skills of the great private companies. This was a handicap with which the British Broadcasting Company, for example, being a governmental institution, did not have to reckon. The Voice has accordingly always been at least in some measure an enterprise of amateurs. It has unquestionably improved, but the major difficulty—encountered like-wise by educational radio and television—which is that of adequate competence in script preparation and technical management, still exists today. It cannot be removed by merely increasing the production know-how.

The challenge now presented by the conquest of space and the resulting feasibility of satellite broadcasting is one which will tax the ingenuity of our technical experts and our cultural leadership. There is something awesome and indeed frightening about the prospect that it will soon be possible to broadcast to half the world from one place at one time, and that the availability of low-priced transistor receivers will prodigiously increase the number of potential listeners. It would seem well worth considering whether the attempt to cope with this new instrumentality ought to be shared in common by the peoples of the Western Alliance, so as to make a centralized impact on the world at large. Already some modest private efforts, notably by the Broadcasting Foundation of America, have been made for the exchange of broadcasts, and these seem to have reaped sufficient success to justify careful and imaginative study.

Libraries and publications

The Information Services began in much the same way as did the Voice. The seedlings initially planted in international soil by the General Advisory Committee on Cultural Relations, as it set about fostering a small number of schools, libraries and cultural centers, were now distributed in huge bundles, particularly, once more, in Germany and Japan. Newspapers and magazines were created and subsidized. Books were translated or distributed in English. But it was the *Amerikahaus* and its equivalent which made by far the greater impact. At least this was the case in Germany. Considered in the tranquil light of everyday intellectual intercourse, the *Amerikahaüser* were not only depositories for literature bearing the imprint of publishers in the United States but also places where those interested, and they were many, could attend lectures, hear concerts, and view exhibits of art. If at first the major emphasis was somewhat tiresomely placed on the virtues and good deeds of the United States, they gradually became civilized places in which the universality of culture was respected.

But perhaps the most notable propagandistic purpose served was to demonstrate the friendly and maybe somewhat lavish manner in which we Americans made reading materials available to the public. One could enter and take from an open shelf books or periodicals which in most parts of Europe were kept behind locked doors and made available only on application. It is of course true that Europeans were not so much being niggardly as making an effort to have the materials in question on hand for all borrowers. American libraries abroad—that in Paris and the Benjamin Franklin Library in Mexico were worthy ancestors of the *Amerikahaus*—are probably among the most effective media through which our culture could be brought to the attention of the world. The "open shelf" principle, to which we have grown so accustomed that we scarcely pay attention to it, is even now something which other nations generally associate with inordinate confidence in the honesty of readers. Yet in some cities today more people read books in the libraries we staff and equip than do so in the similar establishments maintained by the host countries. This is an achievement in which we can take a legitimate measure of pride.

It is a far cry indeed from the small quantity of scholarly literature sent abroad by the Smithsonian Institution at the close of the century to current practice in this field. The number of books and periodicals given away or sold for small sums is great, but even so we have probably lagged behind. It may be said that this is not a business on which the American people embarked with great pleasure. Indeed, they were probably pushed into it. The Nazis gave away an inordinate quantity of copies of *Mein Kampf* and of treatises written by such worthies as Alfred Rosenberg. The Russians have outstripped them. As early as 1951 one could purchase in East or West Germany two leather-bound volumes of Lenin's works for the equivalent of fifty cents. Today the speeches of Khrushchev are cheerfully made available in well-printed editions in all the languages of mankind. We have not done anything quite comparable. With the assistance of American publishers and the consent of authors we have underwritten through contract a very considerable number of books which in one way or other serve a propagandistic or a cultural purpose. The committees of publishers which have advised the government on the matter have rendered excellent service. Perhaps, however, the situation now prevailing needs further study.

The exchange of persons

No doubt the area of the exchange of persons, in which the old Division of Cultural Relations had gingerly set foot, was the one most affected by postwar occupation requirements. The point is of interest because subsequent re-thinking has to a notable extent been occasioned by the experience gained. In 1945 the exchange program was considerably enlarged in order to bring about hoped for inoculations against totalitarian viruses. On the whole, it operated according to its own law of mutuality. Selected Americans were sent to Germany and Japan to meet with groups varied in character in order to convey to them a sense of the values which we strongly believed were characteristic of our society. On the other hand, levies of persons invited to visit the United States were usually selected from occupational groups thought most likely to influence public opinion in their countries.

This activity was certainly not without value, and it is probably regrettable that no reliable diagnosis of its achievements can be made at this late hour. Some things can no doubt be accomplished through carefully shepherded excursions of this kind, even as there is probably something to say for the Intourist methodology. But we have at least one opportunity for comparison. The conferences arranged by Moral Rearmament at Caux, Switzerland, ought not to have been successful, if a variety of American opinions ranging all the way from those of ribald skeptics to those entertained by Catholic and Protestant clergymen are to be credited. But the fact is that they *were*. French-German rapprochement owes to Caux a debt which must be inscribed on the pages of West European history.

Comparative education

The General Advisory Committee had earlier recognized the importance of schools in the cultural program, so it was almost self-evident that in the post-war period the Japanese and German educator would figure prominently among the "exchangees." In the background were academic policies sponsored in the occupied countries on which we shall comment here only to point out that they were transitional between older forms of assistance given to American schools abroad and those which were advocated once the fury of the war had abated. The experience was instructive because it made evident that however impressive our educational achievements may be, it does not follow that our pedagogical practice will automatically impress everyone.

THE COLD WAR AND ITS METHODOLOGY

The cold war soon called for its own methodology and orientation; and perhaps one may say that we of the United States were effective whenever we derived adequate benefit from the occupational experience. To begin with, the cold war immensely broadened the scope of our cultural activity. Then it gave this a radically different character. The Soviet Union was beyond any doubt determined to establish the dominion of communism over the world; and though it was at first difficult for many to believe that this was the case, the grim evidence became more and more overwhelming. One of communism's most thoroughly tested methods was forming elites, usually comprised of unhappy and unemployed intellectuals in disaffected areas, so that through them propaganda carefully tailor-made for the purpose could be widely disseminated. The most effective contention of that propaganda no doubt was that the Russian system was technically the most efficient and at the same time most ardently dedicated to peace. Since there was nothing in the Russian dictator's rule book which imposed an allegiance to truth, it was clear that the only way of dealing with him was to establish the fact that he was wrong and no doubt dangerously so.

Cold War tasks of the United States

Therewith for its own salvation the United States was confronted with three tasks not at all easy to reconcile. The first was to persuade other peoples, among them the former German and Japanese enemies, that safety lay in a common military defensive system to which they must be expected to contribute. This has certainly never been easy. The second was counteracting Russian propaganda on both counts—that is, demonstrating the deep commitment of the American people to peace, and also conveying to needy peoples that this country was in possession of unparalleled technological ability which it stood ready to place, insofar as humanly possible, at the disposal of the peoples needing assistance. The third task was to familiarize other nations with the values for which American democracy stood, even while professing readiness to cherish other cultural heritages in turn. For all these reasons the cold war greatly altered, in some respects revolutionized, the international outlook of the American people and therewith also its cultural relations program.

Certain activities, though they sometimes antedated the cold war, played a notable role in its waging. The International Cooperation Agency (the name has subsequently been altered although the structure of the operation remains pretty much the same) carried out the worldwide commitments of the United States for technical and other forms of assistance. It proved to be the most diversified of governmental agencies, so difficult to survey or evaluate that it would require a staff of research workers to do so with any prospect of success. While many Americans are persuaded, for reasons which baffle analysis, that the Foreign Service Officer is usually a depraved character of minimal intelligence and loyalty to his country, the ICA official merited a special nomenclature providing for all degrees of ugliness. Of him or her it may, however, be said in general that an attempt was made to work to the best of human ability at a job which probably would have had critics speedily out of breath.

Sometimes as in West Berlin we made through ICA quite spectacular contributions to the progress of cultural relations. There a new library, right up against the Iron Curtain, and a complex of student residences built primarily to house young people from the Russian Zone who were bent on continuing their education at the Free University, testify to the occasional munificence and imaginativeness of the program. But most of the time the ICA man was dealing in Worthington pumps, agricultural know-how, and technical skill. Education in the development of technology at all levels has as a matter of fact been ICA's primary concern. Older exponents of a cultural relations policy would probably not have agreed that teaching relatively primitive communities such things as the organization of a street cleaning process was a vital part of what they had in mind. But in the world of the cold war, such jobs must precede what can later on be accomplished through the exchange of ideas.

This last-named form of exchange—the business of explaining what in terms of social and political doctrine the United States believes in and practices, why democratic institutions give a better account of themselves than do others, and how an open society can be created—proves to be very difficult, indeed. If it is to be fruitful, at least two conditions would appear to be indispensable. First, the exchange of cultural values in this sense requires a special endowment of imagination and insight, *on both sides*. We Americans have tended of late to be far too critical of our spokesmen. When one is dealing with groups of foreign intellectuals who have no other deep-rooted desire than to acquire power and who will tailor any kind of ideology which seems likely to serve their purpose, no American, however intelligent, amiable and persuasive, is going to have much success. The second condition is that the teaching of cultural values in terms of the polity must be adapted to social and economic development. The statement is big with meaning, which can only be illustrated here. The two great social facts of our time are the growth of populations in the newly emerging countries and the rush of the surplus from rural areas to cities which cannot absorb them. These are formidable obstacles to the teaching of democratic values.

It must seem that one can only hope for progress in this realm through the multiple action of associations which combine disinterestedness with action. This conclusion seems to have underlain the interesting idea launched by President Eisenhower through the People to People program. He surmised that many undertakings in the area of cultural relations would thrive better if they were sponsored by private citizens rather than by government. A good deal of experience supports this view, and the President could effectively allude to it. American citizens had on their own initiative done such things as sending American books and periodicals to libraries abroad; mailing CARE parcels containing literature and school equipment; arranging for the adoption of cities and towns abroad by their counterparts in this country; subsidizing American studies programs in foreign universities; and making provision for fostering relationships between labor groups in this country and those overseas. Would it not be wise to coordinate, expand and support these efforts? The idea was only partially realized because adequate financing could not be obtained. But it was good nonetheless.

The President continued to be interested in what private groups were doing and in how their efforts could be more effectively coordinated with those of the federal government. A special post of Special Assistant to the Secretary of State was created (December, 1958) for Mr. Robert H. Thayer, one of whose major tasks it was to explore the private sector so as to bring about a meeting of minds among those interested in international cultural activities. In the end, this not only provided a panoramic view of the almost innumerable commitments of private Americans abroad, but paved the way for more effective cooperation between them and the government. The scope of citizen activity in all the countries of the world to which Americans have access is breathtaking. It extends all the way from missionary endeavor by a variety of churches to the modest but fruitful work done by Letters Abroad to encourage correspondence between young people. Then there are any number of organizations diverse in character which have their special missions. And finally there are the great foundations. The fame of some of them is worldwide. Primitive people who go to bed not quite certain where the United States is have the name of the Rockefeller Foundation on their lips. It has helped to remove the scourge of disease, has supported charitable establishments, and has made two blades of grass grow where none did previously. Of late, the Ford Foundation has taken its honored place beside its older sister institution.

CREATION OF INTERNATIONAL ORGANIZATIONS

Meanwhile there had taken place the creation and development of international organizations subsidiary to the United Nations. I have characterized some of them in an article for the *Saturday Review,* and shall borrow a few sentences from that:

> Concerned with the welfare of youth, with education, with the free exchange of dependable information, with the world's food supply and the conquest of disease, they now play a part in the affairs of men incalculably more significant than anyone could have foreseen ten years ago. . . . Nearly all of them engage in education. ILO fosters vocational training, UNICEF is concerned with the teaching of nutrition, WHO prepares leaders in Health Education. But by far the greatest share of the burden is carried by UNESCO, at all levels from elementary and adult education to the secondary school and the university.

Little in our national experience had prepared us for such joint action with other countries. Since the United States abstained from joining the

League of Nations our relations with the International Institute of Intellectual Co-operation, set up under the League auspices, were informal. This was at all times an organization which served the elite. But in 1945 we were called upon to assist in the creation of several bodies which would require of us support for and cooperation with international cultural endeavor.

UNESCO

Since UNESCO is from the point of view of cultural relations the most important of these organizations, our attention will be focused on it. That some kind of international educational agency should be established after the war was strongly urged in several quarters. The men and women in allied governments who were responsible for planning the restoration of education in their countries once the war was ended, naturally thought of such an agency as a source of financial assistance and moral support. Various private groups, on the other hand, desired a consortium of peoples for the purpose of employing educational resources to mitigate the hatreds which then seemed indispensable preludes to war. Moreover, there were scholars, notably natural scientists, who urged joint planning for the efficient exchange of information. The cause—viewed in any light —was certainly worthy.

The Charter of the United Nations was vague as to what the educational agency was to be. But during December of 1945 the matter was threshed out in London at a conference to which the United States sent a strong delegation. The United Nations Educational, Scientific, and Cultural Organization (UNESCO) was created and given a constitution which reflected the mood and interests of the time, though it also determined with reasonable clarity what the powers of the organization were to be and what limitations were to be placed thereon. The over-all objective was to foster peace by bringing about international understanding through education and cultural cooperation. But it was powerless to intervene in the affairs of any member state and could indeed function within any such state only upon explicit and specific request. This mandate was sometimes misunderstood or indeed deliberately misinterpreted.

Implications of UNESCO

Supporting UNESCO meant that the United States was pledged henceforth to enter into a cooperative relationship with other peoples in order to bring about the fostering of education, science and culture in the spirit of the United Nations. Initially, however, there was a disposition to believe that the government should be directly involved as little as possible, and that those who represented it should be men of eminence in their specialties who would be given a relatively free hand. This concept is reflected above all in the manner in which the United States National Commission for UNESCO was formed. The Commission was established by law as a group of one hundred, only a few of whom were to be nominated by the Department, while the great majority were to be designated by private organizations serving the multiform concerns of education in the broadest sense. It was believed that in this manner the triumph of the "grass roots" over bureaucracy would be assured.

But it soon became apparent that this early pattern was somewhat unrealistic. There were several reasons why this proved to be the case. First, more and more countries, with Great Britain in the lead, turned the responsibility for UNESCO over to their Ministries of Education, thus following the lead given by the Allied Council of Ministers of Education during the war. Second, there was a natural though perhaps at first unanticipated tendency on the part of smaller nations to look upon UNESCO as an agency which could help them solve their educational problems through grants-in-aid. These grants might be outright gifts of money or of the services of specialists. The pressure on the wealthier countries could not be kept within reasonable bounds unless governments exercised appropriate diplomatic leadership. Finally, the entry of the Soviet Union and her satellites into UNESCO, some nine years after its establishment, meant the transfer to this forum of the Cold War debate which was so marked a characteristic of the United Nations itself. The Department of State was necessarily compelled to defend its policies through normal diplomatic means.

These difficulties became more obvious as the significance of UNESCO increased. The newer nations began to take stock of their educational needs; and whether the region was Asia, the Near East, Latin America or Africa, the outline of what there was to do resembled a contour map of mountains more formidable than the Himalayas, to be scaled somehow. Soon the United Nations, too, was deeply involved in this startling new adventure of the human mind. Planning became the primary necessity. UNESCO was now not so much a symbol of hope that the world as a whole would see the task as its own, as it was a working partner. More and more money was funneled into it from a variety of sources tapped by the United Nations—Technical Assistance, the Special Fund, the International Development Association, the Inter-American Development Bank. Such an enterprise, farflung in every sense, had to rely more and more on the good will and assistance of the United States, which in turn was of necessity impelled to meet the challenge.

Future relations with UNESCO

There can be little doubt, therefore, that relationships with UNESCO, as of the present and in the future, must play a more important part in the thinking and planning of the Department of State. The responsibilities of the organization will increase; the hopes entertained throughout the world for educational advancement must be supported, and the problems of organization and personnel will require closer attention. Even if the critics of UNESCO were correct, the steps taken in 1945 and 1946, when the first General Conference convened in Paris, could not now be retraced. The organization is so badly needed and so popular in many parts of the world that we cannot any longer imagine what international cultural activity would be like if UNESCO did not exist. One must note also that just as the Department of State has utilized private groups to administer programs, so has UNESCO, and it will doubtless continue to do so, perhaps even more than in the past. The point is of some importance in connection with our own planning.

THE EXPERIENCE GAINED

Before proceeding to consider what the policy of the United States might be during the years which lie ahead, however tentatively we may define those years, we shall summarize the principal decisions reached in the past concerning cultural policy. They are:

1. That the exchange of persons, at all levels of the nation's activity, is a major concern of cultural policy, for the following reasons: it brings about a flow in two directions of personalized information, experience and understanding; it affords the people of the United States an opportunity to acquaint others with the character of our social and cultural institutions; it broadens above all the outlook of teachers; and it emphasizes the concept of freedom in the context of learning.

2. That the concept of freedom is of vital importance, because the function of propaganda, which is formalized and directed learning about a country or a point of view, is of limited value except in times of conflict.

3. That books, periodicals and documentation in forms associated with the term "visual aids" (including radio and television broadcasts) are important resources of cultural policy, especially when distributed in ways which themselves illustrate the character of American life—one such way being the open shelf library.

4. That cultural affairs officers represent the United States effectively and meaningfully when they are truly cultivated persons, above all in the sense that they have expert acquaintance with the countries in which they serve.

5. That the government can in many instances achieve more fruitful results in this field if, even in the area of assistance programs, it entrusts the responsibility for putting programs into operation to private organizations and agencies, since these are less likely to suggest propagandistic aims.

6. That the efforts of private persons and groups in the area of cultural exchange should be encouraged by the government; with the understanding that, when possible, they are to be properly coordinated, without dictation, with what the government itself is undertaking.

7. That international cultural organizations, notably UNESCO, should be vigorously supported because they can in some instances obtain results which no government acting in isolation can expect to obtain, because they are invaluable centers of consultation, inquiry and documentation, and also because, realistically considered, they represent a frugal investment from the point of view of the United States.

All these decisions have now been amply tested and their value has been proved. It is of course true that there is much room for improvement in virtually all respects. But looking back over a period which is barely twenty years in extent, we may say that the United States has made great strides forward in developing a cultural relations policy and program. Admittedly it would probably never have developed had not armed conflict and cold warfare made their impact on the national thinking. Henceforth a new kind of worldwide revolution will unquestionably spur us on to even greater effort. The necessity in which whole continents now find themselves to pass quickly from quite primitive conditions to forms of social living in which urbanization and industrialization will play important roles brings education to the fore as the indispensable prelude to world commerce and understanding. This fact alone will give cultural relations a new dimension.

There are other facts as well. One is the possibility of failure. If efforts to bring about so startling a change in the affairs of new nations should bog down, they will no longer even have the support of the primitive, oral cultures which hitherto have given the lives of masses depth and significance, despite poverty and other ills. Nor in all probability could the deterioration be localized. It would engender conflict and upheaval which might well spread even as the plagues of yore did. Clearly one way to prevent such a breakdown is continued, vigorous and cooperative action by the United Nations.

Political implications of cultural policy

It had become apparent by the time the Congo crisis signaled the end of colonialism in Africa and the emergence on the world stage of a continent of new nations that cultural relations could no longer be shunted off the mainstream of United States foreign policy. One of the principal issues in that crisis was whether the educational system established by the Belgians could be maintained and brought into closer harmony with the nature and aspirations of the independent state which would now enter history. As part of his effort to forestall Russian assumption of leadership in the Congo and a possible war, President Eisenhower sponsored a grant of support to the United Nations for educational and cultural action. This meant, of course, that this action was seen as a vital part of the policy of serving the best interests of the United States through diplomacy.

The administration of President Kennedy immediately took an important step forward by appointing an Assistant Secretary of State for Educational and Cultural Affairs. Consultation was taken with panels of experts to determine the character of what had been and could be done to make the efforts of the United States more effective. Reports of findings were made. More recently (February, 1962), the Assistant Secretary, acting under the authority of the new Fulbright-Hays Act, formed an advisory group, the United States Advisory Commission on International Educational and Cultural Affairs, which to all intents and purposes re-creates the old General Advisory Committee to the Division of Cultural Relations, though to be sure the scope is broader and the means with which to act far greater. In the intervening period a number of other Advisory Commissions had been created, one of which had been the United States Advisory Commission on Educational Exchange which was now superseded.

In 1960 this Commission had invited Dr. Walter H. C. Laves to prepare a report. This is entitled *Toward a National Effort in International Educational and Cultural Affairs* (Department of State Publication 7238). This is warmly recommended to everyone who desires to study in greater depth the problems and opportunities now before the nation. Dr. Laves considers the "general foreign policy objectives" of United States cultural programs:

> Some should be designed primarily to advance knowledge and to strengthen the world community of education, science and culture.
>
> Some programs should be designed primarily to develop an understanding abroad of United States culture and institutions.
>
> Some programs should be designed primarily to develop among the American people understanding of other people and their cultures and institutions.

Some should be designed primarily to make available specialized knowledge and skills to countries at different levels of development.

Finally, some programs should be designed to strengthen the development of democratic societies and other institutions in other countries.

A Theory of Cultural Relations

If this is accepted, as no doubt it should be, as an accurate statement of major objectives in the field of cultural relations, there will be a number of important questions to ask and to answer. Prior to dealing with some of them we may, however, consider with a measure of profit whether a theory of cultural relations can be devised, as distinguished from a pragmatic appraisal of the experience so far gained. Any effort to deal with such a theory must, however, be venturesome and tentative, because no probing study of the problems involved has been made. In the United States one can begin with the sound basic assumption that at the present stage of human history a developed national society tends for the sake of its own stability and welfare to take on an international dimension. We doubtless see this clearly in those areas of activity which are most easily measurable in terms of the national interest. Thus, it is devoutly to be wished that an agreement can be reached with the Soviet Union concerning the control of outer space and disarmament, at least insofar as nuclear weapons are involved. Seen in the light of such developments, extreme isolationist groups in the United States must seem retrogressive. The "international dimension" is inevitable for us because we live in our kind of world.

What is the "international dimension"?

The "international dimension" will of course in many respects not be the same for us as it is for other nations of the free world. We have virtually beaten the United Nations into the kind of ploughshare we need because it could at least achieve a measure of effectiveness as a buffer between ourselves and the Russians. It has functioned at best with a creaking of gears and engines lined with carbon. That some friendly powers have not eyed the scene with exhilaration is understandable. Upon occasion, certainly with good reason, they have watched the process of majority building in the United Nations and its specialized agencies with doubts and misgivings.

We find ourselves in a comparable situation insofar as cultural relations are concerned, though great differences exist. What is the "international dimension" in cultural relations? The answer is, free trade in cultural goods. And what are these goods? They may, I think, be defined

as those accretions of information, inquiry and creative artistic achievement which are the concerns of the modern university. Intellectually
considered, they may conveniently be summarized as the accumulation of
knowledge and method which the human mind has built up around those
fundamental, reality-revealing intuitions which in their totality form the
present outlook of mankind. Thus, in the natural sciences we have developed a great expanse of instrumentalities of investigation and technological achievement around the insights gained by men of genius from
Euclid to Einstein, Planck, De Broglie and Heisenberg. In the study of
society we have moved from Plato and the Mosaic injunctions to the behavioral sciences. Religion, philosophy and the arts have added their own
intuitions and have created around them vast literatures and important
programs of action. With all these the modern university is concerned in
terms of both knowledge and inquiry.

But the university does not exist for its own sake alone. It is the source
from which the lower schools draw sustenance and inspiration. Thus, the
teaching of English literature in a good secondary school today is very
different from what it was a generation or two ago, because university
scholarship has altered both the approach to aesthetics and the contour of
the historical situation in which every book must necessarily be written.
We are all very much aware these days that mathematics and physics cannot be taught effectively unless the teacher comprehends in some measure at least the concepts which now underlie these sciences. To use still
another illustration, the teaching of languages in our time has been radically changed by the application of the findings of linguistics.

Quite as memorable is the manner in which the university has modified
and is modifying the methods of work and the employment of leisure
time. It is not merely that mechanization has been a highly revolutionary
influence, though it has been that to almost an incalculable extent, but
also that in our society at least the working man has been freed from the
kinds of bondage and dependence which were normal a century ago.
This is in part due to the development of social ethics and the social
sciences. Even the mass media, which with us seem anti-intellectual or at
least addicted to circuses, tend in curious ways and normal ones to reflect
the progress of research. Thus, television has familiarized nearly everybody with the weather map, triumph of careful meteorological observation over many years. And, in a different vein, every listener to modern
police reporting and detective fiction will be able to tell you that the
defense attorney in Dostoievski's *Brothers Karamazov* lacked acquaintance with improved techniques in the analysis of crime.

At the level of the university in the strict sense, the "international
dimension" has long since been a routine matter. For example, in former
days, when it was taken for granted that an understanding of the classical languages and literatures was equivalent to liberal education, the
philologists of two centuries toiled to establish texts as nearly perfect

as the most scrupulous study could manage. There was no country in Europe which did not furnish its quota of scholars for the task, and what one did became the property of all. The fact that every advanced student of the humanities was required to know several languages—normally Latin, French and German—also testifies to the fact that scholarship did not stop at national boundaries. For a considerable length of time, research in the natural sciences followed the same pattern. Kepler, Copernicus, Pascal and Newton spoke to their peers wherever in the world these were listening. It was only after the Industrial Revolution and the beginnings of modern warfare that the applications of scientific discovery to manufacturing and armament made secrecy on a large scale the rule.

Today the trend is once again strongly in the direction of exchange. In spite of the cold war, it has been possible for UNESCO, with the assistance of American and British scientists, to sponsor effective international research in geophysics, soil aridity and oceanography. The Russians have effectively cooperated with all these efforts. The tradition of the university has overcome other barriers as well. Exchanges in the field of literature and economics have been resumed on a relatively worldwide scale. Western-oriented countries have gone back since the close of the Second World War to traditional ways of making known the products of research. Indeed—exception having duly been made for the applications of science which are protected by patents or are kept under mantles of secrecy by governments—the sole problem existing at present is how to assimilate what is being offered.

The factors of ignorance and prejudice

But as soon as one comes down from this high perch (it may be noted that members of university faculties are also human, upon occasion distressingly human) there is a different story to tell. We must reckon with the factors of ignorance and prejudice. Let us look at ignorance first. Restrictions on the free flow of information continue to erect mighty barriers between peoples. They are first of all artificially created by governments or private groups. But poverty also plays a part, inhibiting the gathering and dissemination of both news and comment. Many believe that the situation as a whole has deteriorated rather than improved since the close of the Second World War. But there are two other persistent kinds of ignorance. The first is lack of education, which in its worst form may be illiteracy, though in view of what a great many people read one is sometimes inclined to doubt it. The second is specialization, which may so absorb a man's time and attention that his view of the world tends to become one-sided or indeed myopic.

When one has borne these handicaps in mind, it is not easy to be confident that for the great majority of the world's peoples the "international dimension" in terms of cultural relations will soon prove very significant. Yet there are relationships even where we should not expect to find them. For instance, people round the world dearly love to travel, even if they can do so only vicariously by talking with some one who has come from a far country. The magic carpet of the *Arabian Nights* is one of the oldest and best distributed resources of the human imagination. People are attracted by the exotic, provided it remains within what they would consider reasonable bounds. And of course nearly everyone has a bundle of images of certain foreign places, based on sailors' yarns, movies, television and something or other handed down in the family. Paris is a city of sin, Essen is a place where Germans work hard and therefore succeed, Rome is where the Pope lives, and Cairo is full of belly dancers.

The barriers of prejudice are erected close to the images. It is unnecessary to discuss them in detail, or indeed to attempt to isolate the factor of prejudice in the area of cultural relations. But knowledge that it is a world-wide reality, shifting with the times, so that in any society a prejudice may speedily give way to its opposite, greatly affects one's views as to the beneficence of mutual exchange of cultural goods as opposed to propaganda. Prejudice entertained against the United States, for example, is usually rooted in things its citizens have done or are supposed to have done. Tourists have been noisy and obstreperous. Soldiers have misbehaved. And so on. Will all be well if one substitutes people who are models of decorum and wisdom—if one, for example, multiplies Peace Corps contingents? Or will it be desirable to provide a full-dress campaign to advertise the virtues of the American people and thus create a different image?

These are some of the problems with which a working theory of cultural relations will perforce deal. There are others, some of them crucial, for example that of how to utilize the earlier years of education in order to develop a greater readiness to approach other cultures with an open mind. But, if the assumption that an "international dimension" is a plain fact can be considered correct, certain things may be predicted from the American point of view concerning the whole area of life which the university indirectly influences but does not control. First, there will be a certain motivation among peoples abroad to know about the United States, and, conversely, a comparable motivation here to learn more about other countries. Second, having defined the motivation, one can plan more or less realistically to satisfy it. Third, the plan must provide for unity of purpose while projecting the use of highly diversified means.

To attempt a definition of the motivation in question is far from easy. For my part I would say the basic urges are primarily utilitarian but by no means exclusively so. Everyone admires certain kinds of American technological achievement. But unfortunately few other nations consider that our experience in the conduct of government is of use to them. They do not know how to practice our form of parliamentary democracy, and it is very doubtful that they will try hard to do so. An Egyptian will judge Nasser by how well he succeeds in benefiting the rank and file, and not by how he does it, provided he does not resort to wholesale massacre or suppress religion. But there are other urges, too, and some of them are quite different in character.

For example, the fact that the United States has been represented abroad by great philanthropic organizations, notably the Ford and Rockefeller Foundations, has identified this country with unselfish concern for general human welfare. They have carried on a secular program, supplementing in notable ways the activities of missionary groups, which for a long time carried the burden of education in many areas of the world. Efforts as diverse as the struggle to remove the scourges of yellow fever and malaria, the painstaking work to preserve the monuments of Pharaonic culture in Egypt, and the patient development of improved agricultural methods—all carried on without a thought of personal advantage to the donors—have left memories of service and good will which cannot, one thinks, be eradicated. They have formed an image of the American people which is invaluable for us.

National interests and cultural relations

But if one looks at these things more closely, it will become evident that the interests of a culture or a people are always involved. National feeling in Africa is necessarily (though not always realistically) anti-colonial, both because there could have been no nationhood while a colony existed, and because the colonial idea was based on the assumption that the people governed were inferior. And yet it does not follow that the erstwhile colonial relationship, say with Great Britain, will be abrogated in favor of an all-out espousal of American ways or ideas. The new peoples have first of all become used to dealing with the British, to accepting their patterns of education and of speech, and to profiting by often genuinely effective efforts made by the British both to assist the people under colonial rule and to continue that assistance after independence had been gained. The United States is, of course, acclaimed as a source from which economic and technical assistance on a grand scale can be expected. On the other hand, there exist in the United States forms of race feeling which have for a long time not flourished under British rule.

The "international dimension" of the United States is therefore in this instance a two-sided reality. On the one hand, it is not a nation with a colonial past, despite "dollar diplomacy" and temporary imperialist adventures. On the other hand, there is projected from it into the post-colonial world a theory and practice of race relations which summon to mind some of the worst aspects of colonialism. In the long run, attrition may well take its natural course. That is, memories of the colonial past will recede, as they have with us; and the pattern of race relations in the United States will no doubt improve. But at the present time the handicap exists and it is no doubt a serious one.

It would therefore seem that in theory the best way to proceed in some post-colonial countries in terms of cultural relations at the extra-university level would be to accept the reality which the British or others have created and to cooperate with it to the fullest extent possible while taking advantage of every opportunity within reason to foster mutually beneficial exchanges of our own. This would mean less concentration on the anti-communist program and more on inter-Western cooperation. Such activities as Operation Crossroads Africa are no doubt potentially very effective. Nevertheless, in theory, they would be still more productive of desirable results, if it were possible to coordinate them with what European nations are doing. Unquestionably our "international dimension" as a whole is clouded by an excessive concern with communist propaganda and a far too restricted appreciation of the strength of Western Europe.

A comparable situation exists in Latin America. Perhaps the developments in Cuba may serve as a profitable example. It was evident that economic assistance could come from us alone, at least until the Russians began to use the island as a military base. But Cuba had continued, despite the vicissitudes of history, to be in many ways an outpost of Spanish culture. Its clergy, for example, were predominantly Spanish in origin, and the faults of that clergy were probably glaring. No real effort was made to recruit a native priesthood. The fact that Castro was an illegitimate child continued to be emphasized during his early years. Meanwhile, of course, the Spanish revolutionary tradition had influenced the outlook of those who were opposed to the established dictatorship. Had we not been again so certain that economic assistance would create a favorable international view of the United States, we could have taken steps in time to supplement the cultural impact of Spain on Cuba with forces which might well have prevented the debacle. For instance, were we not so obsessed with the separation of Church and State where Christians are concerned (we can collaborate with Islam in Pakistan without batting an eye), we could very probably have greatly affected the position of the Cuban Church as an ally. Much more could be said.

In Latin America as a whole, our economic and strategic interests have often been opposed to those of the native populations. As a result, in the area of cultural relations, "freedom" from their point of view has generally been something radically different from what it has been from ours. We have coveted a free hand in banning European influences we considered undersirable, in conducting business and investing capital, and in fostering spiritual and intellectual movements reflecting our own cultural pattern. But when the Latin American has conjured up the notion of freedom, he has thought in the first instance of a long history of military actions taken by his neighbor to the North. He has remembered the Mexican War, the Spanish-American War, the building of the Panama Canal, and the punitive expedition set in motion by President Wilson. The two conceptions have clashed over a long period and have of course led to a measure of exploitation, real or fancied, and on the other hand to the confiscation of capital investments. Regardless of who has been right or wrong, older attitudes still underlie the otherwise very impressive structure of international cooperation which has more recently been erected.

Therefore when we speak of the free exchange of cultural goods, we must see to it that both Latin America and we understand the terms the same way. Otherwise the ship will sink before the cargo leaves port. Many young Latins come to the United States in quest of an education, and profit by it. Many more study English—indeed, English will very likely become the second language of Latin America. But actually the amount of cultural exchange and its quality leave very much to be desired. In one respect we try too hard, perhaps, and in another not hard enough. Anxiety to keep Latin America safe for ourselves and the free world is a highly laudable emotion. We should have begun to feel it sooner. Unquestionably, sending young Americans to Chile as members of the Peace Corps was an excellent idea, but, just as certainly, inviting a comparable group of young Latin Americans to come here would be equally commendable. The Latin American university has little to offer us in the natural and social sciences. But it does have much in the humanities and the arts.

The free flow of cultural goods

One may state by way of summary: motivation in the area of cultural exchange derives from the conviction that the free flow of cultural goods will be to the advantage of the participating peoples and states, though it may not immediately affect other interests of a political or economic character. This conviction is supported by an almost universal belief that education is a blessing in which all the sons of men can share. Yet there are special things to say about it. While politics and economics are tested and served by action—in free states both private and governmental action—and to a limited but still important sense by propaganda, the free flow of cultural goods will be most effective when it exists for its own sake. To be sure, it will be benefited and not hampered by what may be termed effective salesmanship. Common sense dictates, for example, that when exchange fellowships are made available, they should be given to the grantees with as few commitments as possible. The accepted reason should be that those who obtain them will have an opportunity to see and learn as much as possible of what they *wish* to see and learn. Nevertheless, the mere fact that the scholarships are offered is propagandistic in character and must be recognized as being so.

Since, as has been said, cultural values are, for the most part, the products of the university, conceived of now in the broadest possible sense, it is important to see what it is that the university's objectives are. One may answer that ideally it is committed to the unhampered and fearless confrontation of man with reality, and that therefore it is the most powerful force which can be pitted against ignorance and prejudice. At all levels of education or human experience which it controls or influences, it desires the largest possible measure of conformity with its own spirit. But we must be realistic and add that in the present world situation the university can also unfortunately be an instrument or a slave. The communist university, whether in Russia or the satellite states, is in important areas of thought restricted to a program of indoctrination. It must teach the social sciences not as they are, but as the government of the Soviet Union desires them to be. Nor can the arts, philosophy or religion be discussed with an open mind. Consequently, we need to assume, when we as citizens of the United States undertake to promote or share in the free flow of cultural goods, that we must act in the spirit of the great, traditional university of the West, and that as a result "propaganda" for it, overt or implicit, is an essential component part of the action.

"Propaganda," however, must never ignore the essential issue: what is needed and desired is freedom of inquiry and of choice. Accordingly, the stream must always move in two ways. Cultural relations can be effective only when minds *meet*. An American university in Cairo will prove worthwhile and beneficent if those who teach in it learn to know Egypt even while imparting specifically American kinds of knowledge. Operations Crossroads Africa will succeed only as those who comprise it acquire insight into the country they are serving.

If what has been said about motivation in the realm of cultural relations and about the complex situations in which it functions is accepted with at least a measure of assent, two things follow: first, the program as a whole must be designed to promote a free flow of cultural goods at three levels—that of the education of the trained elite, that of the formal teaching of the schools, and that of what is termed adult education; second, each single effort must be carefully planned and just as carefully put into practice. Concerning the first, it may be said that while it may not always be possible to work on all three levels, none can be neglected in theory. There is often a tendency to ignore one or the other on the basis of assumed principle. Thus our cultural programs, both public and private, tended during the period between the two World Wars to concentrate on the trained elite. Most of them were as a matter of fact the endeavors of the learned societies acting with some measure of government support. After 1945 there was a tendency to assume that only an effort to reach the "grass roots" was any longer realistic. Of course, there was a great deal to say in favor of both positions. Let us as a consequence accept both.

The problem of coordination

One may then proceed to say that while a measure of coordination of what is done by government with what is achieved by private groups is desirable, and that accordingly while the efforts to that end made by the Department of State are to be commended, it is gravely to be doubted that government ought to attempt to set up any sort of plan with the expectation that private citizens or groups should be controlled by it. I am of course not speaking here of these when acting as agents for the government, nor can there be any question that coordination is upon occasion imperative. Good examples are the manner in which Hungarian students were assimilated by our institutions of higher education, and, more recently, the intervention of the Department of State to rescue African students from the near disaster in which many of them found themselves when private adventures in student exchange broke down. Normally, however, the free flow of cultural goods will be assisted if private initiative and indeed tradition are given free rein. Some confusion and some duplication of effort must be anticipated, but the plain fact of the matter is that no government agency has either the time or the omniscience which are needed to draw up an over-all blueprint for everyone to follow.

But government should have a blueprint for its own activities, which should be projected as far into the future as is at all possible. It should take into consideration all of the various instrumentalities of cultural exchange, and should bring these into a desirable alignment. Thus, for example, cooperation with UNESCO should not be put into one cubby hole while the United States Information Agency is placed in another, but rather as much cross reference as is at all possible should be effected. It is far more important that the government's efforts should be coordinated than that these are put into one package with private endeavors. In 1962, the most difficult task of coordination is that made necessary to provide more educational personnel and facilities for the developing countries. It is of course true that this effort to assist schools must form part of the work to be done in promoting economic and social advancement. But care must be taken not to subordinate it to such an extent that it ceases to be truly part of an educational plan.

Granted the unity suggested, it will soon become apparent that each project needs to be endowed at all times with its own individuality. If a program is to succeed in France, it will have to be designed for France. And yet one cannot any longer think of that country without bearing in mind that it is now placed, more than ever before, in a European context. In like manner, if something really effective is to happen in Africa, it must be planned for some region or state in particular, even while the continental dimensions of the total African effort are borne in mind. This is extremely difficult to do. There are doubtless not nearly enough people available to get the job done. And so it may be asked whether, at this stage in the planning, it might not be wise to use the services of experts from abroad just as we have employed them in atomic and rocket research.

Summary

At any rate, this is a tentative theory of cultural relations which can no doubt be greatly improved. It may be restated briefly:

In our time, every highly developed country has taken on an "international dimension" which means interaction with other countries and regions.

The "international dimension" in cultural relations is the free flow of cultural goods. These are essentially the concern of the modern university, either directly or through the lower schools and the instrumentalities of mass education and public opinion.

The obstacles to the free flow of cultural goods are primarily artificial curbs of cultural traffic, ignorance and prejudice. These are formidable obstacles, but there exists a powerful motivation to surmount them.

This motivation is the product of a conviction that a free flow of cultural goods, to and fro, will serve the individual nation's interests, sometimes directly but also upon occasion indirectly.

These interests will be best served if as far as possible the spirit of the university, which is that of the unhampered and fearless confrontation of man and reality, is conserved. But in view of a divided world it cannot always be conserved.

So much being taken for granted, it follows that the cultural relations program of the United States must have a unity of objective but a marked diversity and flexibility of approach.

The unity should be sought not through an impossible endeavor to bring public and private efforts into some kind of artificially created bundle but by cross-reference between the great variety of government activities, correlated as fully as possible with private effort.

By diversity is meant the realistic, well-informed adaptation of each activity to the target with which it is concerned.

Two General Problems

We shall, in the light of what has been said, consider very briefly two general problems which government must face when it acts in the dimension of cultural relations. The first is the problem of adaptation of personnel policies; the second is the problem of exchanges.

Adaptation of personnel policies

It is fairly obvious that when we think of cultural relations we must bear in mind both our country's involvement on its own initiative, whether voluntarily taken or enforced by reason of the international situation, and its association with other countries already at work in a given area. With some of these countries we might well seek to cooperate, while opposition to others will prove unavoidable. In other words, there are practically no parts of the world in which we can find and expropriate virgin territory. Second, it should be apparent that cultural relations activity in a country with an old and rich literary culture will have to assume a character quite different from that of a program to be carried out in a country which is still close to an oral tradition, or has perhaps wholly lost a sense of tradition. In both instances a considerable measure of tact is required; and tact—apart from being a mysterious something one either has or doesn't—may be defined as adequate orientation for the task involved.

Manifestly not everyone who represents the United States on a cultural mission will have the experience or the receptivity which would ideally be required. Yet it is very important that some should. One cannot expect the average lecturer, exchange student, technician or even Fulbright scholar to be more than his nation has equipped him to be. But our country needs to provide, in intimate association with them, at least one or two persons who serve as symbols because they are accepted as equals and friends by the cultural leaders of the countries to which they are sent. This does not mean that they are to associate only with the elite. On the contrary, in some countries a professor who speaks the language may make the greatest impact on the common people generally. Finding such men and using them is a difficult task, particularly since the Foreign Service is not organized to recruit them or to use their services over more than brief periods of time. Cultural relations are from the career point of view far from being competitive at present either in interest or importance with the conduct of diplomacy serving the major political or economic interests of our country's advancement.

Another major difficulty is the mobility of the Foreign Service, and still another the mantle of security every officer must constantly wear. No sooner has a man prepared himself well for a cultural mission and thoroughly familiarized himself with the life of a country than he is whisked off the premises and sent to a wholly different part of the world. The mantle of security which must be worn if the diplomatic business is to succeed is for its part a grave handicap because if a Foreign Service officer consorts too freely with aliens he may inadvertently find himself in water no longer lukewarm.

No doubt the general provisions governing the Foreign Service cannot be changed in any notable way. But it might be interesting to consider whether the category of Cultural Attachés could not be so established that it would depend upon its own recruitment procedures and also have a promotion and advancement schedule of its own. This last might be comparable to what prevails in academic life. Were this done, the Department might also find it possible to deviate from the normal rules of rotation and so allow a good officer to remain in the country with which he is familiar for a longer period. If all this were once agreed upon, it should prove easier to enlist the kind of men and women needed for the task, and map out careers for them which would be equal in terms of rewards of several kinds—intellectual as well as monetary—to what they could have earned in the American college or university. A cultural relations program will be no better than are those appointed to carry it out. Changes in method or increases in the amount of money or materials made available will not in the long run achieve the objectives sought unless the people to whom the mechanism is entrusted are genuinely first-rate. This truth remains important also when there is question of those who are to do the everyday chores associated with various kinds of cultural or assistance program. Most of them will be on short-term assignments, and what matters, therefore, is their ability to carry out these while not doing harm. The number of those so employed is growing steadily, which almost automatically suggests that the quality cannot be uniformly high.

The whole problem and the data on the basis of which it can profitably be considered have been outlined in a number of publications, two of which will be singled out here: *Americans at Work Abroad* and *The Overseas Americans,* by Harlan Cleveland and others. The points of view expressed in these volumes cannot be brought into focus here, but the reader will encounter verities which probably had to be accepted during the earlier stages of the foreign aid or mutual assistance programs, and which should slowly but surely be restudied. A large number of American citizens are now employed either by the United States government or by private organizations and foundations. Some of these have been or are obviously misfits. This is not at all surprising, nor is it peculiarly American. Not everybody who is employed by a college as an instructor survives the period of initiation. Nor, strange as it may seem to perusers of some currently popular literature, is every Russian who goes to a foreign area an exemplar of tact, ability, morality and plain common sense.

But, as the authors of a valuable survey of the situation and of the pertinent literature, Frank N. and Helen G. Trager ("Exporting and Training Experts," in the *Review of Politics*), have indicated, some steps can no doubt be taken to bring about improvement. One is in recruiting. In all probability, the government tends to overrate the factor of youth and to discount maturity. There is, of course, not a little to be said in favor of the policy so far in force. First, the young can *probably* cope more effectively with the climatic and other hardships encountered on some missions. On the basis of personal experience, I rather doubt this; and I suspect that a careful review of missionary history would support the legitimacy of the question mark. Second, it is very likely true that on the whole men and women past forty-five are so firmly rooted in what they are doing that it is often difficult, indeed, to pry them loose for foreign service. Yet it would seem that there are sources of supply which could be tapped, particularly for personnel who are to remain on a mission for some time.

Another change called for is in the process of orientation. At the present time, Washington normally supplies four weeks of instruction, which is beyond all doubt desirable but which must in the very nature of things be inadequate. It follows, therefore, that some additional orientation in the country of assignment ought to be provided. It might well be worth considering whether in areas where programs of some size and duration are contemplated, a center of orientation should not be set up wherein veterans from the United States and carefully selected native educators or officials would join forces during an additional four weeks to prepare recruits for effective work.

The exchange of persons

The important and central question of the exchange of persons came of age insofar as the government is concerned with legislative acts which retain in this area of activity a significance comparable to that of the Land Grant Legislation in the history of our educational system. The Fulbright Amendment, which was the expression of an imaginative approach to the problem of restoring cultural ties that had been broken off as a result of the Second World War, was followed by the Smith-Mundt Act and, more recently, by the Fulbright-Hays Act, which greatly enlarges the scope of cultural relations. These are impressive illustrations of how the importance of cultural exchanges has been understood by the Congress.*

There are several ways in which the problem involved can be formulated, and we cannot review all of them. It must suffice to indicate the basic reason why anybody is interested in going to another country to study is that he can, or at least thinks he can, learn something he would not if he stayed at home. He may be mistaken, or what he has in mind may be of trivial value, but the target is of sufficient interest to induce him to take the trouble. In large part, *directed* cultural exchange is a matter of identifying things which ought to be learned about, and then finding people one thinks can and will learn them. That, for example is pretty much what happens when the Ford Foundation establishes a program of fellowships for foreign study.

In view of the relative ratios of development, between, say technology in the United States and scientific illiteracy in Liberia, directed research in our time must often be heavily weighted. That is, we set out to learn, broadly speaking, *about* some peoples, and they learn *from* us. Neither process is easy. The first may be qualitatively more difficult, but the second is from the quantitative point of view vastly more exacting. It is said, for example (though one may not wish to vouch for the accuracy of the computation), that ninety per cent of all scientists who ever lived are alive now. But why are they alive now? Because a very great deal of time, money and talent have been expended on building up institutions in which scientists could be trained and given opportunity to do research. Obviously by comparison, sub-tropical Africa, where only a single university owns a nuclear reactor, has to learn from us, or from other countries comparably experienced and staffed, if it hopes to add significantly to the number of scientists. And this again will cost a great deal of time, money and talent.

Learning about a country is hardly a science but an art. Learning from a country is hardly an art but a science. To expound this difference would require a volume, were it to be attempted with the requisite thoroughness. We shall merely note that there are, in the main, two ways of learning to know a country. The first is through making a careful study of some aspects of its history, customs, physical characteristics and institutions. The second way is to study the culture—or perhaps one should borrow a term from psychologists and say the *Gestalt*—of a country so thoroughly and imaginatively that one comes to see it from the inside. One may

* The Fulbright Act of 1946 provided for the use of foreign currency balances accruing abroad for mutual cultural exchanges. The Smith-Mundt Act of 1948 provided limited dollar support particularly for foreign scholars coming to the United States, the total amount available being determined annually by the Congress. The Agricultural Trade and Development and Assistance Act of 1954 earmarked funds accruing abroad from the sale of surplus agricultural commodities abroad for exchange purposes. The Fulbright-Hays Act of 1961 very considerably broadened the exchange program but no provision was made in this Act for funds with which to implement it.

then still be mistaken in estimating the course it will take historically, by reason of irrational and other factors—but one's errors will be those of the people one has come to know and not those of an outsider.

The second consideration, namely that some countries seek to learn from us, was discussed by the then Assistant Secretary of State for Educational and Cultural Affairs, Philip H. Coombs, in a significant and intelligent address entitled, "Let's Talk Sense about Foreign Students," delivered before the 14th annual meeting of the Greater New York Council for Foreign Students, Inc., on December 4, 1961. This describes a number of basic concerns so well that it should be read by everyone interested in the subject. Undoubtedly, insofar as students who study here are concerned, the basic question is what can they do with what they have learned when they return to their native lands? For if the answer should be "Nothing," the futility of the whole effort would have been demonstrated. Mr. Coombs said:

> For his own country and for ours the returned foreign student represents an important investment and asset. We know that in many, many individual instances these "assets" are put to highly productive use. The lists of what returned Fulbright scholars are doing to serve their fellowmen are most impressive.
>
> But there are many other cases in which the student returns home and fails to find a good opportunity to put his newly-gained skills and knowledge to good use, especially in the less-developed countries.
>
> There are many complex reasons for this and it is not a problem which can easily be solved. But it is vitally important that every effort be made to gain progress in this direction. . . .

These are observations of moment because they highlight one of the most complex areas of cultural exchange. On the one hand, it would be of interest and value to compare our experience with that of the French and the British, both of whom also have a considerable stake in helping post-colonial peoples to learn what they must if their societies are to prosper. How, for example, would the British Commonwealth scholarship program compare with our Fulbright program in terms of the eventual contribution made by returning grantees? In theory it would seem that those in the British program should be more successful by reason of experience gained in the area. On the other hand, the question of what happens to students returning from the Soviet Union raises important and difficult questions of another character. If, as is perhaps to be assumed, the Russians continue to keep a watchful eye on young men and women who have studied in Moscow, and if indeed they do not fail actively to subsidize them, what questions would such actions present for the government of the United States?

*   *   *   *   *   *

What has been said may suffice to indicate that cultural relations are, insofar as the United States is concerned, at a stage of development which will require the very greatest intelligence and even venturesomeness, the term being admittedly new. I have employed it to symbolize what seems to me the key to the future, namely cautious but vigorous experimentation. The United States has come a long way in twenty-five years. But it must move faster and farther. Perhaps in our planning for the future, we should also reckon with the tremendous increase of cultural relations activities which would take place if disarmament were in large measure achieved.

W. McNeil Lowry and Gertrude S. Hooker

2

The Role of the Arts and the Humanities

The arts have never been the property of a whole nation or race, and something is risked when they are employed for social or political reasons. Ideally, intercultural mobility should emerge as a manifestation of the vitality, pervasiveness, and needs of the arts and the artists themselves, without reference to foreign policy, but in a society which at the same time sees the artist as a representative of some of its most conscious values. In sum, if we put this conception of the arts at the top of the scale and attempt to justify the expenditure of public funds, we must drop down through several philosophical levels before we come to the assumptions hitherto accepted for United States international cultural activities. From ideal to actual, the planes would arrange themselves as follows:

W. McNEIL LOWRY *is Director of the Ford Foundation Program in Humanities and the Arts. Between 1953 and 1957 he directed the Foundation's Program in Education. A one-time member of the faculty of the University of Illinois, he helped to found and edit* Accent, *a quarterly of new literature. During World War II he was a writer in the Office of War Information and a Lieutenant in the Navy, and afterwards was Chief of the Washington Bureau of the Cox Newspapers. In 1952-1953 he was Associate Director of the International Press Institute and supervised the study of the flow of international news in India, the United States and eight European countries.*

GERTRUDE S. HOOKER *is on the staff of the Ford Foundation Program in Humanities and the Arts. She was Associate Editor of* Common Cause *between 1946 and 1949. Dr. Hooker was with the Cultural Affairs Division of the USIS in Rome between 1951 and 1959 and in Paris between 1959 and 1961.*

1. Spontaneous intercultural movement as a manifestation of the vitality and pervasiveness and needs of the arts and of the artist, without reference to foreign policy.

2. If such movement could not be spontaneous, but required public or private funds, then the use of such funds without reference to national foreign policies.

3. Public funds to use the arts as media by which to illuminate and reflect the Western ideal of the supremacy of the individual.

4. Public funds to reflect abroad a particularly American view of man, wherever it exists.

Note that the arts are put at the top of the scale, and that even the last, the most constrained of the four objectives, does not assume that activities carried out to express it, can (in the language of the Fulbright-Hays Act) "assist in the development of friendly, sympathetic, and peaceful relations between the United States and other countries of the world." But why should the arts be put at the top of any scale when the subject is cultural activities and their relationship to United States foreign policy? The answers must here be given as short articles of faith.

One article is that what art is about is not what foreign policy is about. Art may easily suffer when it is used, as it often is, for nonartistic purposes. And if there is a question whether even good artistic exchange contributes to peace, and there is such a question, then perhaps we ought to assume that bad artistic exchange is not a good risk for United States foreign policy.

Another is that only when we begin with artistic considerations may we expect the support of the artists and artistic directors, and that without that support we again risk a bad exchange at both ends of the transaction. Art may or may not be mysterious, but the processes and techniques by which it is produced have often eluded the most powerful, the wealthiest, and the most determined men.

Indeed, there are direct corollaries between this intellectual argument and the ways in which the arts should be used in relation to foreign policy. We are concerned with *why* the arts are thus used; we must be equally concerned with *how*. And the point is that the farther we move from an ideal situation in which intercultural movements spontaneously manifest the vitality and the needs of the arts themselves, the more we need to cling to strictly artistic considerations when we are attempting to use the arts for other large purposes.

To keep artistic and political values most nearly in proper relation, government activities in the international cultural sphere should be managed directly and indirectly to:

1. Support art, the artist, and cultural activities for their own importance in the society.

2. Use the strictest criteria of artistic excellence in the choice of artists and artistic groups employed; or

3. Employ those talented artists and artistic groups who will in the process be assisted in their professional development.

4. Help to improve public taste.

5. Profit from the intensive and realistic advice of artists and artistic directors themselves.

6. Ensure, by means of the above principles, the moral and intellectual support of the artistic community at home and abroad.

PURPOSES OF CULTURAL EXCHANGE

Government-sponsored cultural activities overseas in the past decade have not been based upon artistic considerations and only partially upon general political motives such as upholding the idea of the supremacy of the individual. Instead such activities have been based on the assumption that they would increase understanding and acceptance of United States policies and institutions.

When the American Assembly studied the question of cultural activities overseas in the symposium on *The Representation of the United States Abroad* in May, 1956, Mr. Howland Sergeant, former Assistant Secretary of State for Public Affairs, deplored the lack of "a clear, understandable United States government policy as to the role of these cultural relations in our national policy." In a brilliant exposition of information and cultural representation overseas—still largely valid—he resorts constantly to such adjectives as *muddy, complex, cloudy,* and *fuzzy* in trying to explain the relationship of cultural programs to foreign policy objectives as well as to the much more clear-cut information program.

A few weeks after he took office, President Kennedy called attention to the purposes of cultural and educational exchange programs when he observed that "the whole field was in need of imaginative policy direction, unification, and vigorous direction." A few months later, in September, 1961, passage of the new Fulbright-Hays' Mutual Educational and Cultural Exchange Act invited and demanded a rethinking of the whole political and moral philosophy behind the programs.

The act itself defines the purposes of cultural exchange in very broad terms. It is intended to increase mutual understanding . . . , to strength the ties which unite us with other nations by demonstrating the educational and cultural interests, developments, and achievements of the people of the United States and other nations, and the contributions being made toward a peaceful and more fruitful life for people throughout the world; to promote international co-operation for educational and cultural advancement; and thus to assist in the development of friendly, sympathetic, and peaceful relations between the United States and other countries of the world.

Behind these unexceptionable intentions lies a whole cluster of more or less related and compatible purposes.

Cultural competition among nations

Historically the United States was the last of the major nations to engage in government-sponsored cultural exchange, and its original motive was defensive. When the Division of Cultural Relations was established in the Department of State in 1938, its activity was limited to Latin America and its purpose was to counter Nazi and Fascist cultural propaganda in the Western hemisphere. Ever since, this negative approach has colored and often dominated official thinking and planning. When the Cold War has been intense, cultural diplomacy has been difficult to justify to the taxpayer except in terms of a contest or a race with what the communists were doing. The magnitude of the communist effort to reach the intellectuals has often obscured the fact that virtually all the advanced countries—no less than 35 in 1958, according to a recent UNESCO report—carry on cultural and educational activities abroad as a routine department of foreign relations, for a great many reasons both idealistic and practical.*

* Detailed information on current programs of a number of countries appears in the *Hearings* on S. 1154, pp. 159-62. The Government of the UNITED KINGDOM spent an estimated $65 million on combined information and cultural activities in 1959. The British Council had offices in seventy-two countries, including six in Germany and Nigeria, five in Iran, and four in Italy, India, and Pakistan. (See *Annual Report of the British Council,* 1959-60.)

FRANCE had cultural attachés in virtually all of the eighty-odd French diplomatic missions abroad, some forty French cultural institutes and thirty-three French cultural centers in some fifty countries throughout the world.

The GERMAN FEDERAL REPUBLIC is estimated to have spent about $13 million for cultural activities under the Cultural Department of the West German Foreign Office, including the cultural centers, libraries and schools; language instruction, teachers and study materials; cultural exhibits and performances abroad; and academic and leaders' exchange programs.

ITALY has an extensive program in some seventy countries and uses all types of media. In 1959, thirty-four cultural institutes in twenty-eight countries ran 133 libraries and

The mission civilisatrice

The idea that cultural activities overseas have a "civilizing mission" has also traditionally been quite alien to American (and British) thinking, and it is only recently that our responsibilities toward newly-developing countries have raised the question with some urgency. Both British insularity and American isolationism, in their different ways, reflected a complacent state of mind about the excellence of their native institutions and way of life and the assumption that if other peoples did not wish to imitate us, so much the worse for them.

The French approach for many decades, or indeed centuries, has been very different. Herbert Lüthy traces the French missionary idea back to the Crusades and the noble Christian ideal of the *gesta Dei per Francos*. In any case, because France sees herself as the guardian of human civilization itself, she has at all times engaged in a dynamic campaign of "intellectual expansion" aimed, as we read in the 1960 Report of the Foreign Office, at offering other peoples, especially the young, the "formation" that comes with mastery of the logical and practical instrument that is the French language, and hence "the means of attaining a source of spiritual as well as material riches."

The needs of newly developing countries

What the French have long known, and what we have only recently begun to recognize, is that there exists a large consumer demand for cultural commodities in other countries. Although this market is by no means limited to the lesser developed areas, its intentions are described with particular clarity by spokesmen for the new countries of tropical Africa. "Even when we have solved this problem [of colonialism]," wrote Leopold Senghor recently, "there will still be another problem—that of the choice between civilizations in contact; we shall have to see what we shall take from Western civilization and what we shall keep from Negro African civilization."

In the last few years, as the priority objectives of United States foreign

---

reading rooms, held lectures, showed films, etc. Somewhat similar activity on a higher cultural level was carried on by 119 branches of the Dante Alighieri Society—a private organization which is assisted by the Government—in thirty-five countries.

A number of Latin American countries maintain token information and cultural programs in foreign countries.

For a report of activities of the Sino-Soviet bloc countries in 1960, see *Hearings*, pp. 165-209, where detailed statistics on exchanges appear. The most comprehensive general treatment of the *Soviet Cultural Offensive* is by Frederick C. Barghoorn (Princeton University Press: 1960).

See also *Directory of National Cultural Relations Services* (UNESCO: 1958).

policy have shifted from the postwar reconstruction of occupied countries through successive phases of the cold war to the present major concern with the growth of new and developing countries, cultural exchange has been called upon for a corresponding variety of contributions. In the early stages of the Point Four program its role was marginal, and limited to such matters as technical assistance in developing crafts as a resource for the local economy, or printed instructional materials. There seemed good reason to hope, especially with the Marshall Plan analogy in mind, that direct economic assistance along with precise technical training could give the necessary leverage to these countries, and do so in a short period.

It has become increasingly evident that simple economic betterment neither satisfies the aspirations of these peoples nor does it lead to the kind of "manageable instability" that is required for democratic institutions to evolve—in fact the appeal of the communists has been strongest in the field of material development. "Fortunately for us in terms of our competition with the communists," wrote Lloyd A. Free and Hadley Cantril in a report prepared in 1957 for the Rockefeller Brothers Fund:

> man is much more than an economic unit. It is not without significance, for example, that the strongest aspiration of all among former colonial peoples has been, not economic betterment, but political independence. Actually, the intensive nationalistic feelings of the people, even after they have won independence, have caused them frequently to act quite contrary to their own economic interests (as witness, for example, the Indonesians forcing out Dutch enterprises upon which the livelihood of many depended; the Burmese refusing the United States assistance they sorely needed; the Syrians sabotaging the pipelines upon which their national economy is dependent; the Jordanians renouncing a dependable British subsidy).

> In fact, economic betterment, alone and by itself, occurring within the framework now existing in many areas, may actually worsen the political situation and increase the danger of communist subversion at least temporarily. By permitting the people to lift up their heads to new desires and aspirations, partial economic betterment may actually augment frustrations and discontent —unless it is accompanied by the political, social and psychological evolution in democratic directions necessary to give the people hope for the future founded upon confidence in their political, economic and social systems.

Among the non-economic needs of the new nations, national cultural identity is a principal ingredient of political independence, and is often of very high significance. As Walter Laves has noted in his recent report on educational exchange activities, "It sometimes represents the one national asset which establishes them on a footing of equality with other countries, counterbalancing to some extent the economic and other deficiencies of which they are acutely aware."

The needs of the American people

Just as the new countries are adding new dimensions to the meaning of cultural exchange, so the worldwide rapid pace of change made it logical for government cultural programs to contribute part of their resources to a better understanding of foreign cultures within the United States. This too is a revolutionary development.

The new Fulbright-Hays Act is called the *Mutual* Educational and Cultural Exchange Act, and it makes possible a number of new reciprocal exchanges. It authorizes the use of government funds not only for bringing foreign creative and performing artists and athletes to the United States, but also for interchanges of handicrafts, books, translations and international expositions demonstrating cultural attainments, and other related purposes. Since it is only now going into effect, it is premature to predict how it will work, or even whether funds will be allocated to it, but there are suggestive precedents in other countries.

France and Italy have long conducted cultural exchanges on the basis of reciprocal agreements, whereby art exhibits, for example, are exchanged, with each country paying the cost of the visiting exhibit within its own territory. Though the intention could be to share costs equally, the arrangement pleases and flatters other countries and no doubt contributes to the reputation of Paris as the world center of refined taste in the arts. The Soviet Union, in spite of withholding royalties, has for years won friends among foreign writers by translating their books systematically, often into several languages and usually long before other countries had discovered them, if indeed they ever did. Another example is that of the French-writing poet Leopold Senghor, who was published in Czechoslovakia in 1947, many years before he emerged as President of Senegal. It is not unlikely that this contributed to Senghor's pro-communist political views prior to the Hungarian revolution.

There will be many difficulties in carrying out the "reverse flow" provisions of the new act. An obvious problem is the lack of a central official source in Washington with whom the foreign ministries can deal, and which would have the authority to handle visiting manifestations with appropriate official fanfare.

Increased understanding abroad of United States policies and institutions, cultural competition among nations, aid to the development of newly independent nations, better American understanding of foreign cultures—these have been the chief purposes upon which United States government activities were based until 1962. The passage of the Fulbright-Hays legislation in 1961 has also led many persons to expect a more general, and less political, attention to cultural relations abroad. There is as yet no assurance of this development.

The American cultural resources used by public and private agencies overseas have chiefly been motivated by the objective of increased understanding of United States institutions and policies.

Utilization of United States Cultural Resources

Musical arts and artists

In government exchange programs in the arts, musical artists have been the most active. Between 1952 and 1961 the United States government awarded grants to 1189 persons specialized in music. Of these 900 were Americans, of whom 700 went overseas to continue their training. Some have returned to distinguished careers in American musical life: the 1961-62 roster of singers at the Metropolitan Opera includes seven former Fulbright students. Meanwhile young American singing talent continues to fill the opera houses of Germany and Italy with what has been evidently their richest source of supply.

The flow overseas of mature concert soloists has increased so notably in the last decade that artificial stimulus is usually unnecessary. The Department of State steps in only to extend commercial tours to countries or areas off the beaten concert path: for example, to send Eugene Istomin or Isaac Stern to Iceland, Rudolf Serkin to the Far East and India, Joseph Fuchs to Latin America and the Far East. A few concert artists are beginning to reach tropical Africa: William Warfield pioneered in British West Africa in 1956, followed by Camilla Williams in 1958. In French tropical Africa the principal musical ambassadors have been Louis Armstrong, the Golden Gate Quartet, and the Westminster Singers. In the new countries the volume of musical traffic is limited not only by costs but sometimes by the lack of a suitable hall or even a piano.

American composers have also participated regularly in cultural exchange, and many of the major ones have been sent abroad by the government. Private foundations such as the Martha Baird Rockefeller Fund, the Guggenheim and the Rockefeller also provide opportunities for musical talent to work abroad. The American Academy in Rome gives hospitality to several young composers annually. Concerts organized by USIS provide recognition and experience for the young artists; USIS lectures and recorded concerts go on around the world, according to the energy and imagination of individual USIS officers.

If the musical artists, especially at the student level, have been conspicuous abroad, notably in Germany and Italy, overseas tours of American symphony orchestras are still a comparative rarity. The New York Philharmonic is the most widely traveled, having made European tours in 1955 and 1959, visited Latin America in 1958, Greece-Lebanon-Turkey in 1959, and Japan in 1961. The Philadelphia Orchestra has gone twice to Europe; the Cleveland Orchestra once. The Boston Symphony visited Europe in 1956 and the Far East in 1960. Latin America has been toured by the National and New Orleans symphonies; the Far East by the Los Angeles and Symphony of the Air; the Near East by the Minneapolis Symphony. In 1958 western Europe was also toured by the Juilliard student orchestra, whose professional training surprised and pleased many critics; in the spring of 1962 the Eastman student orchestra had a similar reception.

The average cost to the Department of State of an overseas tour of a symphony orchestra is over half a million dollars or about one-fourth of the annual budget of the cultural presentations program. At the present level of appropriations, it is impossible to send more than two orchestras a year, and thus even major foreign capitals are unlikely to have more than one concert at intervals of several years.

Other very costly tours have been those of *Porgy and Bess* (1955), *Oklahoma* (1955) and *My Fair Lady* (USSR, 1960). Until recently the high cost has ruled out opera altogether. In 1961, however, the Santa Fe Opera received limited assistance to perform at the Berlin Festival and in Belgrade: along with two Stravinsky works, it presented Douglas Moore's *Ballad of Baby Doe*. Otherwise foreign music lovers have had no opportunity to evaluate the condition of opera in the United States except marginally, e.g., at the Spoleto Festival, or through the performances of American singers on their own stages.

Mention should also be made of government-sponsored performances abroad of several chamber music ensembles and choral groups. Benny Goodman, the Robert Shaw Chorale and a number of other musical artists visited the USSR under the exchange agreement. In the summer of 1962 an American high school choir (from Princeton, New Jersey) went to Europe for the first time with partial government assistance.

Other government programs involving music include the United States Specialists program (see below) and the various USIA media—collections of records and printed music, background lectures, documentary films such as *The Tanglewood Story, Design for Music* (a recent Lincoln Center documentary on Philharmonic Hall, narrated by Leonard Bernstein) and others on Marian Anderson's tour of the Far and Near East and that of the Boston Symphony in Japan.

Examples of international musical exchange and cooperation under private initiative are too numerous to report in detail and have been multiplying in the last few years. The Tanglewood festival has imported major European figures fairly sytematically for many years. There has been increased cooperation among European and American opera houses in sharing the cost of new sets: the Dallas opera, for example, has brought over Franco Zeffirelli and the sets he designed for La Fenice in Venice. A number of American conductors have been working at intervals in the

Far East, training orchestras and investigating the Oriental musical idioms. Examples might be multiplied.

Some Results of Musical Exchanges—This description suggests a great deal of activity, and probably musical artists are happier than their colleagues in other fields about the opportunities and the things that are happening to stimulate musical life. And yet, when the government resources are divided among one hundred-odd countries, it turns out that in many parts of the world American performing artists are rare indeed. USIS officers in Southeast Asia and Latin America, for example, report that American music is represented too often by second- or third-rate artists; composers complain that their works are virtually unknown abroad, even in Europe; another frequent comment is that too many grants go to young artists who could receive as good or better training in the United States, and should have it before they appear on European concert stages. It is also noted that the cultural presentations program is smaller than that of the British or the French, and that we have not systematically tried, as France does, to promote the works of native composers. Although United States government grantees are required to include some American music on their programs, composers note that the American number may be a very short one such as Barber's "Adagio for Strings."

Government-sponsored tours are run on exceedingly parsimonious budgets which have to be supplemented by private subsidies, ticket sales and so on. Commercial performances abroad rely on box office receipts to the maximum extent feasible, and the cost of tickets often discourages many music lovers.

Perhaps the most interesting by-products of postwar exchanges in music are seen in the recent contacts between East and West. In 1961 the East-West conference in Tokyo symbolized the fact that Japan is now one of the world's great cosmopolitan music centers; that it has a wealth of symphony orchestras (six in Tokyo alone) and an enviable supply of talented string players, a number of whom have won awards and acclaim in the United States. Later in 1961, following the visit of the Juilliard Quartet, plans were developed for a summer music camp in Japan, similar to those at Tanglewood and Marlboro, where young Japanese musicians (and perhaps those from other parts of Asia) might work with American teachers.

Among Americans who have been particularly active in disseminating knowledge of Indian music, the work of Alan Hovhaness, Howard Boatwright and William Malm has attracted particular attention. Mr. Boatwright recently published a textbook on the system he has devised for adapting Indian music to the Western five-line staff notation; Mr. Malm is the author of *Japanese Music and Musical Instruments*. Meanwhile in the United States the University of California at Los Angeles has become a leading center of study and performance of the music of Japan, Indonesia, Iran, India and China, and held its first festival of Oriental Music and the Related Arts in 1960. The Rockefeller Foundation has made grants to UCLA for this activity, to assist purchase of Asian instruments and research materials as well as for study opportunities for both Asian and American musicians.

Theater

The condition of the American theater must be judged overseas almost exclusively by the plays and playwrights. Miller, Wilder, Williams, O'Neill—and all the distinguished American authors—are not only household names among theatergoers abroad, but indeed victims of not infrequent unauthorized performances and pirated editions. In contrast to this lively circulation of the leading American plays, the state of the American theater is otherwise impossible to appraise since so few companies have as yet attempted overseas tours.

United States government efforts are still in a rudimentary stage. The first pilot project was sent out in 1956, when *Teahouse of the August Moon* toured five Latin American countries. The following year the Department of State made a major effort, but limited chiefly to Paris and the Théâtre des Nations, which was then in its first year. In connection with the "Salute to France" the Department partially subsidized performances of *Medea* with Judith Anderson, Wilder's *The Skin of Our Teeth*, and O'Neill's *Long Day's Journey into Night*. University drama groups have been used abroad sporadically since 1957; and in 1962 a Drama Advisory Committee was appointed to attempt to use more artistic criteria in their selection. In 1959 and 1960 no American theater company went abroad under the government program. In 1961, more than a million dollars of the cultural presentations fund went to a quickly organized Theatre Guild American Repertory Company to present three contemporary plays: *The Skin of Our Teeth, The Glass Menagerie,* and *The Miracle Worker*. This group, headed by Helen Hayes and Leif Ericson, visited 24 cities in Europe and the Near East, and another dozen in Latin America.

Apart from the few government tours, American companies have generally been unable to venture abroad. The Actor's Workshop appeared at the Brussels World's Fair, and the Living Theatre has been to Western Europe twice after strenuous and only partially successful fund-raising campaigns.

If one contrasts this modest record with the annual theatrical manifestations abroad under French government auspices, the relative impact of American offerings appears to be slight and fleeting. In 1960 alone, for example, according to the annual report of the Direction générale des affaires culturelles et techniques, the Comédie Française toured West-

ern Europe; the Vieux Colombier Eastern Europe and the USSR; the
Théâtre National Populaire went to Argentina; the Renaud-Barrault
company visited the Middle East and Japan; and another classical repertory troupe under Max Palenc brought Racine and Molière to eleven
cities of the Belgian Congo, with stopovers elsewhere in Africa.

An important experiment in "reverse flow" took place in 1960, when
the first full Kabuki repertoire company came to the United States and
brought to audiences in New York, Los Angeles, and San Francisco what
Brooks Atkinson called "pure theater that does not imitate life, and con-
sists of ritual, ceremony, style and spectacle." Although the Japanese
government and Japanese private industry assisted the New York City
Center in subsidizing the tour, ultimately the Rockefeller Foundation
also had to step in.

The most important international theater festival is the annual Théâtre
des Nations, held every spring in Paris. The idea emerged from the 1955
meeting of the International Theatre Institute in Dubrovnik, and the
Festival got underway in 1957. During the 1962 season 23 nations participated (as against 19 the year before) in 41 different performances,
the largest program to date. Since its inception, the Théâtre des Nations
has presented most of the world's greatest theater, from the Berliner En-
semble and the Berlin Opera, to the most distinguished companies of
England, Italy, Ireland, Greece, the USSR and many others. United
States participation has been haphazard, except for the first year. Since
1957 the only government-sponsored companies have been the Helen
Hayes repertory theatre and the New York Pro Musica *Play of Daniel* in
1960.

Otherwise, United States activity in the theater has mainly been
personified overseas by individuals. Under government exchange programs some 250 Americans in theater arts have gone abroad to study,
teach, or do research, and over 200 foreign grantees have come to this
country; Fulbright grantees from American university theater departments have participated in or initiated theater seminars, readings or
performances from Finland to India. In 1961, Margaret Webster visited
South Africa on a Specialist grant where she gave Shakespearean recitals
and directed Eugene O'Neill's *The Touch of a Poet*. In 1960 Hal Holbrook's one-man show, "Mark Twain Tonight" toured ten countries of
Western Europe. There are no statistics on the many others who travel
privately, but perhaps it is significant that of seventeen American theater
directors who recently received Ford Foundation grants for their professional advancement at the particular career stage they had reached, the
majority chose to observe directors abroad.

The Rockefeller Foundation has given modest assistance to work in
drama in various parts of the world. In 1960 it made four grants to individual Latin American theater directors and artists to observe activities
in the United States; funds were also appropriated for the first time to

support theater in tropical Africa—the Ghana Experimental Theater in Accra.

Dance and ballet

Of all the performing arts other than concert music, ballet has been most adequately represented overseas. Three principal United States companies have toured abroad several times under the cultural presentations program: Lucia Chase's American Ballet Theatre, four tours, including Latin America, Europe, the Near East and Africa, from 1955 to 1960; the San Francisco Ballet, three tours, including the Far East, Near East, Latin America and Africa, from 1957 to 1959; and the New York City Center Ballet which went to Europe in 1956, the Far East in 1958 and the USSR and East and West Europe (fall, 1962). In 1959 Jerome Robbins' *Ballets USA* toured Europe, Poland, Yugoslavia, Israel and Greece arousing storms both of praise and criticism. In the dance field, Martha Graham toured the Far East and Near East in 1956; Jose Limon has appeared twice in Latin America and once in Europe and East Europe. No American ballet or modern dance company has yet visited countries of central Africa, although the Bolshoi ballet has been there.

Visual arts, artists, exhibitions, museums

A paradoxical state of affairs emerges when one attempts to analyze what is happening overseas to American art and artists. On the one hand, of all the artists, it is the painters who have won the highest distinction on the international scene—recognition from Paris and London that the style of painting most in vogue in New York today is, or was until yesterday, the most exciting and influential in the world. On the other hand, organized government activity in the arts has been halting and spotty and capricious in the extreme.

The federal government's program of touring exhibitions got underway shortly after the Second World War. It ran almost immediately into a storm of criticism from many of the citizens' groups which in a democracy insist on monitoring all aspects of government activity. There is not space here to review the various chapters of the often dramatic and astonishing tale: suffice to say that the government has been cautious, and sometimes paralyzed altogether. It is not surprising that USIA, which has responsibility for art exhibitions, has done a minimum of reporting on its activities.

In spite of the obstacles, several fairly large exhibitions have gone abroad in the last few years under government sponsorship, chiefly to Europe. Among these were the exhibition of 19th century American painting which toured various European countries; the collection of

French paintings in American collections *De David à Toulouse-Lautrec*; another, *French Drawings From American Collections,* shown in Rotterdam and Paris; *Twentieth Century Italian Art from American Collections,* shown in Milan and Rome; and the recent exhibit of *American Painting of the Twentieth Century* sent to Moscow. During the year 1962, USIA has had the *American Vanguard* exhibit—a collection of 88 contemporary paintings—in Yugoslavia, Austria, Germany and London; along with a very few small collections of paintings elsewhere (14 to Santiago, for example, for the Pan American Art Festival; and 5 to northern Europe). But the principal emphasis of late has been on graphic arts and prints, which are obviously less expensive to handle, less difficult to display, less controversial, as well as highly distinguished for intrinsic artistic merits.

As is apparent, the government's own program has been minimal and in recent years steadily declining. USIA's budget for fiscal year 1962 allowed only $3,500 for Washington support of art exhibitions, for example, though actual expenditures were in the vicinity of $20,000.

Chief responsibility for presenting American art overseas has been carried by the Museum of Modern Art, with principal support from the Rockefeller Brothers Fund. For many years the Museum has handled United States representation at the two major international biennials in Venice and Sao Paolo, where such artists as Pollock, Rothko, Marin, Shahn, Calder, Kline and others have come to the attention of the world's leading art critics. In April, 1962, the Museum announced that it could no longer afford to sponsor these activities; it reports that its outlay for handling the last thirteen exhibitions has been some $265,000 plus an estimated $250,000 in curatorial time, use of museum space and the like.

The combined resources of American government and private activity do not add up to those of other governments. Again looking at the French example, one notes that in 1960 a total of forty-two art exhibitions, comprising 5,800 works of art, traveled abroad to eighteen countries. In selecting works for export, special emphasis was placed on contemporary painting, sculpture, printmaking, tapestry and decorative arts.

Meanwhile interest in American art overseas has never been keener. A high official of the French government complained recently that the United States had had no major exhibition in Paris since 1955, in spite of frequent invitations from French authorities. "It is true," he added thoughtfully, "that there is no need to foster better friendly relations between our two countries, but I think there *is* room for progress in getting to know each other better. . . ." In London in the spring of 1962, where USIS presented the American Vanguard exhibit in the Embassy, the *New Statesman's* critic called attention to the fact that "the number of paintings by De Kooning, Still, Gorky, Kline, Newman or

Hofmann previously shown in London in no case adds up to double figures, and that none of them is represented in a public collection here." He added ironically, "De Kooning may be the most influential painter now working," but London "has had a glimpse of no less than nine of his paintings over the last six years."

If this has been the volume of artistic traffic to Paris and London, what of other world capitals? In Latin America, the last comprehensive exhibition of contemporary American paintings took place in 1941. In Japan, showing of American art has been more frequent but hardly representative. The chief sources of information in Tokyo have been art magazines, word of mouth, a certain number of one-man shows by American artists in residence there, such as Sam Francis and Bernard Childs, and since 1952, the International Exhibitions sponsored by the newspaper *Mainichi Shimbun,* which have been held at regular two-year intervals.

At the first of these exhibitions thirty-nine American works were displayed, including those of some of our best-known artists; over the following ten years American participation has been increasingly spotty and unbalanced with only prints shown, for example, in 1959. However, in May, 1962 it was reported that a major exhibition of 100 contemporary American paintings was scheduled to visit Tokyo and one other Japanese city late in the year, with sponsorship of the Museum of Modern Art, the USIA, and the People to People Program. If the American experience is similar to the French, this may prove to be the most successful art exhibit sent abroad in terms of numbers of visitors: French government officials report that the exhibit of *L'Art français 1850-1940* sent to Tokyo in 1960 attracted 1,500,000 visitors and has been to date the outstanding event of the French government program.

A number of efforts are being made apart from touring exhibitions. Among these is the collection of 2,500 slides on American arts and crafts assembled with assistance from the Carnegie Corporation and designed in part for deposit in libraries and institutions abroad. The Ford Foundation is currently supporting a series of monographs on living American artists intended for dissemination overseas as well as in the United States. Another Ford program is assisting American art museums in the preparation of annotated catalogues of their collections—a need that has often been stressed by art critics and connoisseurs abroad. USIA over the years has subsidized translations of books such as John Baur's *Revolution and Tradition in American Art*; it has promoted diffusion of French and Italian editions of *New Art in America,* and occasionally presented other art books to institutions. An imaginative pilot project set up recently by the Museum of Modern Art provides outstanding works of art for ambassadors' residences abroad on a circulating loan basis.

Some 633 Americans have received government grants in the last ten years to study and work abroad in painting, sculpture and the history of art; another 304 foreign artists and art historians came to the United States. The majority of these awards have gone to persons concerned with art history and scholarship rather than to creative painters and sculptors. A number of former Fulbright grantees in painting and sculpture have, however, won major honors.

Among institutions participating regularly in intercultural exchange, the Smithsonian Traveling Exhibition Service has been active since 1952 and handles most of the foreign exhibits in the United States, usually in cooperation with the embassy concerned. The American Association of Museums carries out a small but growing international program. In 1960, with State Department assistance, it organized the first of its annual regional tours for invited foreign professionals (10 in 1960, 17 in 1961 and again in 1962), who subsequently attend the annual meeting of the AAM and have an opportunity to meet colleagues from all parts of the United States and Canada.

Private foundations have also recently begun to make small but growing grants for the development of the arts, crafts and museums in lesser developed countries. The Asia Foundation has since 1955 given recurring support to the Kabul museum, and made occasional grants to arts centers and museums in the Philippines, Taiwan and Japan. The Asia Society and Japan Society of New York have for many years brought exhibitions of oriental art to this country. In 1961 the exhibit of Chinese national treasures from Taiwan was an outstanding event.

The humanities

Contacts between humanists in the United States and those in other countries since the Second World War have been numerous, but less organized, than contacts in other fields. Except for American studies, United States government support has been limited and spasmodic. Through the senior Fulbright appointments, many American humanists have spent some time abroad, chiefly in the fields of history and literature. Many more have traveled under grants from foundations.

One of the major postwar academic developments has been the organization of area studies, especially those relating to Soviet Russia, the Near East, Southeast Asia, the Far East, Africa and Latin America. Many American scholars have traveled and studied abroad in connection with these programs, a few with government support but the great majority under grants from the Ford, Rockefeller, and other foundations. In numerous instances these grants have been made by the American Council of Learned Societies, the Social Sciences Research Council or by universities themselves, but the funds for these grants have come chiefly from the sources mentioned.

At the same time, the United States has made many contributions to the studies of these areas in foreign countries, again chiefly through grants by the Rockefeller, Carnegie, and Ford Foundations. The conclusions of the Scarborough Commission providing for university support of area studies in the United Kingdom were reached after travel of members of the Commission in the United States under the Rockefeller Foundation. The large program of area studies of the 6th Section, École Pratique des Hautes Études, Paris, followed visits to the United States by Professor Fernand Braudel and several colleagues under Rockefeller Foundation grants. The support of area studies at Nuffield College and St. Anthony's College in Oxford owes much to the Ford and Rockefeller Foundations. Similarly, Soviet and Chinese studies in Japan were aided by fellowships and travel grants of the Rockefeller Foundation. Very recently a number of Ford Foundation grants for African studies, in tropical Africa as well as in the United States, have potential political as well as cultural significance.

Contacts in other fields of the humanities, notably linguistics and philosophy, have been frequent, although not usually systematic. The spread of English as a second language, (to which foundations as well as the government have contributed many millions) and the study of descriptive linguistics, are responsible for many contacts involving scholars from Egypt, India, the Philippines, and Latin America.

In 1958 the Ford Foundation granted funds to the American Council of Learned Societies and the Social Sciences Research Council for a program to encourage international scholarly congresses in the humanities and social sciences to meet in the United States. At that time only one international congress of special concern to the ACLS and SSRC membership had met in the United States since World War II; since then American scholars have been able to play host to their foreign colleagues in musicology and history of art (1961) and in sociology and history of science (1962); arrangements are underway for congresses in anthropology, plastic arts, and other fields. Until the last three or four years, the principal obstacle to the holding of such meetings in the United States was the stringent visa policy imposed by the Congress, which unfortunately for many years antagonized and alienated numerous foreign scholars and intellectual leaders.

The most extensive program involving foreign scholars have been those in American studies, supported both by private and governmental funds. The term "American studies" is still in need of a clear definition at home and is often equated with an interdisciplinary approach typical of area studies in general; but in the intention of the few persons in the Department of State, USIS and certain foundations who have been working to encourage American studies, what is meant is university-level study of American history, literature, fine arts, and political institutions on a par with the formal attention given to these disciplines of other countries. At this early stage, American history is the field which needs the most attention just as it has been the most neglected by foreign historians, with few exceptions. Here one encounters the massive opposition of the traditional European approach to education, whereby the entire field of twentieth century history is almost ruled out, and American history is only an incidental casualty—notably the case in France, where the "fifty-year rule" keeps students of history from access to any archives after 1912.

In spite of such obstacles, the number of courses in American history and literature given overseas in the last decade has been steadily increasing, and a movement which started in Western Europe had spread by 1960 throughout most of the world, with courses in history as well as literature being offered in India, Japan, Peru, Pakistan, Iran, Argentina, etc. The Salzburg Seminar, also with foundation support, has long provided another stimulus to younger scholars through intensive one-month seminars.

In December, 1960, the Ford Foundation made a five-year grant of $2.5 million to the American Council of Learned Societies for the encouragement of American studies in Europe, and this may contribute significantly to solving such problems as the need for course materials and travel and study opportunities for the slowly growing nucleus of mature scholars who are doing specialized work on American institutions, thought and history. It is not yet certain whether American scholarly interests will be able vigorously to attack what has been and still is the principal barrier for European scholars interested in American studies: the lack of adequate research materials and of a great research library in the field, somewhere on the continent. Although books and overseas libraries have received a great deal of attention on the part of both government and private initiative, as we shall now see, the central problem—by no means insoluble—remains to be faced.

Overseas libraries

Books and libraries are at the heart of government cultural programs overseas, just as the library is the focal point of the cultural or information center. In June, 1962, USIA had 181 information centers operating in 80 countries, supplemented by another 85 reading rooms and small book collections. In addition, another 145 binational centers, chiefly in Latin America, contained collections of books and periodicals. Most of the USIS libraries average 10-15,000 volumes, although they range in size from the Berlin *Amerikahaus,* with more than 50,000 volumes, to the 1,200 volume basic collections in new libraries in Africa.

The USIS library is usually the chief or the only source of American books overseas for the average reader and even for most university students. Only in Paris is there an important private American library, open to the general public, but it is small by the standards of an American university library. USIS libraries consist largely of current books and periodicals and government publications, along with translations of American books into local languages, wherever available.

For several decades American foundations have made grants to foreign universities and libraries for the purchase of collections of American books. In spite of these continuing efforts, the demand seems to be inexhaustible. USIS too has made presentations to institutions—chiefly books on American literature, history and culture—but at no time have funds for this purpose (always vulnerable in Congressional eyes) been adequate to allow for more than token activities. In the last few years they have declined to a world wide total of $148,580 (1962 estimate) for presentations both to individuals and institutions. Some of the university contracts of the Agency for International Development (formerly the International Cooperation Administration) have included funds for initial gifts of books for specialized subjects in the relevant field. In India, for a few years, the Wheat Loan bill made it possible to purchase annually about $500,000 in books for Indian libraries, but this source has fallen off. Finally, numerous private organizations and individuals have provided voluntary books and services, from CARE and the well-established United States Book Exchange administered by AID to the sporadic and often counterproductive efforts of citizens' book drives across the country.

Sales of American books overseas

It is difficult to obtain reliable facts or even opinions about the availability of American books in bookstores overseas. Export of books and printed materials has multiplied ten times since the Second World War, more than that of any other country. The development of the paperback industry has obviously increased the market for good paperbacks as well as the others. But the United States publishing industry, unlike the British and the French, has not been either proficient or greatly interested in the export market, and even in most European countries professors and scholars who know what book they want have to order it from the United States.

The United States government has tried to remedy this problem, wherever dollar shortages were the cause, through the Informational Media Guaranty Program. Since its inception in 1948 as part of the European Recovery Program it has been generally acclaimed and has been a model for similar schemes of other governments. In the last few years many publishers have deplored the fact that the IMG program has steadily declined, and by May, 1962, was operating at an all-time low of $4.9 million and in only eight countries (Poland, Yugoslavia, Turkey, Korea, Afghanistan, Pakistan, Vietnam and Indonesia). USIA, which administers the program, has requested an increase to $7,175,000 in Fiscal

Year 1963, to allow for expansion into additional countries, perhaps including Latin America. Since the beginning of the program, 55% of the IMG contracts have been with book publishers, with magazine publishers receiving 20%, motion picture producers 22%, and miscellaneous printed materials such as maps 3%. Future plans call for a higher percentage to book publishers, and stronger emphases on text and reference books of a scientific and educational character (which already receive 41% of IMG contracts). English-teaching texts will receive first priority.

USIA Low-priced Book Program—This government program, undertaken in 1957, aims to meet a variety of needs in the Near and Far East and Africa. "Student editions," selling at ten to fifteen cents, are exact reprints of books on American art, biography, fiction, government, history, medicine, science: a recent listing of 126 titles now available includes such entries as the *New Pocket Anthology of American Verse* edited by Oscar Williams, autobiographies of Andrew Carnegie and William Allen White, *Ethan Frome,* and selected short stories of Henry James, along with *The Soviet Regime* by W. W. Kulski and books on science and technology for general readers. "Ladder" editions are designed for neo-literates in English and include books of the same general type but with basic vocabularies of 1, 2, 3, 4, or 5,000 words. Also under this program come abridged student editions and translated editions. A new USIA program handled from Paris is beginning to produce French versions of the "Ladder" series for countries of tropical Africa: 27 books were underway by May, 1962, and plans called for greatly accelerated output. In general, USIA hopes to expand its low-priced book programs from the estimated $462,800 in 1962 to $869,000 in 1963. Editions average from 10,000 to 25,000 copies. Primer-type biographies of leading Negro figures, for example, are included among works selected.

USIA Textbook and Translation Programs—USIA utilizes foreign currencies accruing from the sale of surplus agricultural commodities under the Agricultural Trade Development and Assistance Act of 1954 (Public Law 480, 83rd Congress) to finance "the translation, publication and distribution of books and periodicals, including government publications, abroad." By the end of 1960 currencies were available in 22 of the 26 countries with which bilateral agreements had been signed and textbook programs were underway. By May, 1962, 53 titles had been published in 12 languages in 13 countries, chiefly scientific textbooks, although in France and Italy textbooks in the humanities—especially history and political science—were predominant. In Italy 15 volumes of a 20-volume series of "Classics of Western Democracy" had appeared.

PL 480 has provided significant assistance to government translation programs—sometimes in the absence of any other funds for this purpose, but it has also been a notable example of how government funds become available in a haphazard way.

In addition to this special activity, since 1950 USIA has promoted the translation and distribution abroad of American books "which illustrate important aspects of American life and culture or which contribute significantly to the exposure of Communist theory and practice." By June, 1961, some 6,215 editions had been published in 50 countries. Most of these are published complete and unabridged by established commercial publishers, with the Agency assisting through partial subsidy of the costs, often through advance agreement to purchase copies for libraries and presentations. (Similar arrangements are made by many foreign governments: France, for example, has recently undertaken a textbook translation program into Spanish for use in Latin America.) In some of the countries of Asia, condensations have been published. In the earlier years a fairly high percentage of funds went for books about communism; in general the translation program has had to conform, like all USIS activities, to the objectives of the "country plan" and thus long-range planning to meet lacunae in the various disciplines has been difficult. But a number of American classics have appeared; for example, *The Federalist Papers* in many languages, usually for the first time. An outstanding series of classics of American history has been underway in Italy for several years, with the advice of members of the Harvard Committee on American Civilization.

Franklin Publication—For the past ten years, since June, 1952, Franklin Publications has assisted the publication of an additional 1,300 books, chiefly in Arabic and Persian, but with a growing output in Urdu, Bengali, Malay, Indonesian and the Pushtu language of Afghanistan. As a non-profit private corporation, Franklin has received financial support from foundations, corporations, individuals and governments (United States and other). With its headquarters in New York it has worked closely with the publishing industry, notably in providing technical assistance in the development of a strong local book industry. Since the beginning, Franklin has stressed its reliance on local initiative and support, official and professional, and it has enjoyed other advantages of continuity. A check of titles published indicates that they are generally identical with books supported by USIA in similar areas, with the exception of a few long-term and costly projects such as a Persian dictionary, supported by the Ford Foundation, an English-Arabic dictionary assisted by the Rockefeller Foundation, and translations into five languages of the *Columbia-Viking Desk Encyclopedia,* with assistance from various sources.

"Reverse flow" translation programs

In the past decade there has been growing awareness of the need to make more of the literature and thought of other countries available in the United States. In 1952 the Rockefeller Foundation made a first grant to the Modern Language Association for an inquiry into the role that foreign languages and literature should play in American life. In 1959 the Rockefeller Brothers Fund initiated a program for translations from the literatures of Asia being carried out by the Asia Society. Last year the Rockefeller Foundation made a similar important grant to the Association of American University Presses for encouragement of translations of Latin American writings.

These combined efforts do not match activities in publishing and translation in the Soviet Union, which have become so astronomical as to defy interpretation. One reliable source reports that 40 million books in foreign languages were published in 1960 largely for distribution in the underdeveloped countries. Included were textbooks strictly devoid of political content, books for children, a number of works of contemporary Soviet novelists, along with Marxist classics. The most frequent languages were English, French, Spanish, Arabic, Hindi and Bengali in that order. In addition to translations exported from the USSR, an additional Soviet publishing effort goes on in many countries locally, of substantial if unknown proportions.

Proposals for increasing the flow of books

In the face of all the pressures, it is universally agreed that both government and private achievements to date have fallen far short of needs and responsibilities. When a State Department task force met in June, 1961, twenty-seven discrete proposals were made. "One of the most important problems of all," wrote one highly experienced observer, "is the integration of activity within the United States. One problem has been that we have literally dozens of programs dealing with American books overseas. . . . There is little coordination among these activities." Even among the principal government agencies involved, he added, there is an evident discrepancy in purpose and policy. "The people who have been most active in the use of books—the USIA—have seen them as instruments of persuasion rather than as tools of development. The people concerned with economic development have thought of books only marginally and if they have used them at all have done so for only temporary projects. There has been no concentrated planning." This comment, one might add, takes into account only two of the purposes of books as an instrument for cultural exchange.

Of all the resources at our disposal, books are surely the most precise and eloquent instrument of all. In many ways, they are the least costly and most enduring of the communications media. To date our utilization of books, and significant periodical literature, is still rudimentary. The government effort appears increasingly directed toward neo-literates and the use of books as a tool for development. Commercial exporters are primarily concerned with subliterary products for a universal public interested in entertainment. No sustained effort is yet meeting the needs of the international intellectual community on whose solidarity real understanding depends, and for which books are the most vital need of all.

PROBLEMS AND OPPORTUNITIES

The foregoing pages have shown some of the principal examples of exchanges in the arts and the humanities over the past decade or so—a substantial amount of activity which nonetheless falls well below the optimum in both quantity and quality. The one truly positive development in these years has been the growing public and congressional support. This enlarged base of support has been strongly assisted by the now considerable reservoir of former exchangees and cultural emissaries, government and private, who have experienced the stimulation and challenge of direct contact with other cultures, who have sensed the failure of communication and its intrinsic significance. A great deal of re-evaluation has been going on in an effort to sort out the resources and liabilities of the United States, to find out how these look to others and to ourselves, and to keep up with change which has been remarkably accelerated at home as elsewhere.

The first peculiarly American liability in cultural exchange is also, paradoxically, an asset. That is the very fundamental handicap of the confused and contradictory state of American critical opinion as to the merits and defects of American culture. If there are identifiable, purely American artifacts and institutions, which are they? What is the national character, the "national style"? When foreign observers try to isolate what is specifically American in the amalgam, they fall back on the American Indian, with jazz, the Negro problem and racial discrimination also coming at once into focus. American critics may go to the other extreme and find European sources so recondite and pervasive that little identity remains.

But it is also an advantage that American culture is a descendant of the entire Western heritage. It should be possible to communicate in many different artistic and intellectual idioms. The process of assimilating and importing the best of European and other cultures has been intense since the mid-thirties, with few interruptions. In all artistic fields (except creative literature) the flow of foreign talent to the United States, especially to New York, has probably been unequaled in any other major capital.

Another resource of which the United States possesses unprecedented wealth is the whole apparatus of communications media and techniques: the English language to start with, the techniques for mass production of

cultural materials and especially for distributing them, and above all
the mentality which assumes that it is desirable and profitable to reach
as many consumers as possible. We are in a position, at least potentially,
to export or re-export the best products available.

The rapid spread of English in the postwar period has been a surprising phenomenon, which originally was not officially contemplated or
fostered. To be sure, the British Council has long recognized the central
importance of language teaching, just as France has always been equally
clear about the key significance of the French language as an introduction to French civilization and influence. But the United States has
been caught short by the spread of English, and government English-
teaching programs overseas are only now "tooling up," amid a critical
shortage of teachers. The demand for reading materials and films seems
inexhaustible and is so obvious that for the past decade the Soviet Union
has also been publishing extensively in English.

Language is an asset of unprecedented potentiality; it also entails
heavy responsibilities. Countless observers, foreign and American, are
concerned about the nature of the "unprogrammed" exports from the
United States, in English, and opinions are often apocalyptic. We may
know less than we thought we did about the ultimate psychological impact of these offshoots of popular culture on overseas consumers who are
not intellectuals, as their American consumers are not. In any case, most
of the myths and prejudices about American culture overseas are to be
traced to foreign intellectuals who, we assume, are not the consumers of
these products of mass media.

Bureaucratic difficulties

One generalization frequently made is that the resources of our communications machinery—government and private—have not been used to
their full capacity for exporting the *best* products of United States and
Western thought and culture. Virtually every commentator on government programs stresses the recurring need to keep quality in mind, as do
innumerable field officers concerned with cultural affairs. Obviously many
factors which militate against this goal are endemic in government operations and well known: the haphazard origin and financing of many
programs, irresistible pressures to spread resources too thin, the im-
possibility of long-term planning on the basis of one-year appropriations,
the confusion of purpose which results when these programs attempt to
serve simultaneously all foreign policy objectives, the inevitable shifts of
emphasis that accompany the constant movement of foreign service personnel, and so on.

In addition to, or perhaps because of, these conflicting influences,
USIS operations overseas have since about 1955 been markedly decen-

tralized. The policy was intended to encourage superior quality through closer cooperation with local populations and sensitivity to their needs, but the disadvantages have now begun to impress various observers. Just as American business overseas has recently been shifting to a policy of "recentralization," so the latest Annual Report of the United States Advisory Commission on Information recommends that "communications within the Agency, presently weak, should be better both in Washington and in the field and between Washington and the field. Overseas personnel report that they feel themselves increasingly isolated from Washington." Similarly, Robert E. Elder in his recent report on *The Foreign Leader Program* finds that excessive delegation of initiative to the field prevents effective planning and evaluation. The ineffectiveness or inactivity of the various advisory committees concerned with arts and letters stems at least in part, in the view of some observers, from their lack of authority or influence. Although too much centralization and "masterminding" is also undesirable, and may be the more normal danger in a large bureaucracy, nonetheless the very broad mandate of a government cultural exchange program permits a most heterogeneous assortment of activities—unless there is constant evaluation of what is worth while and what is activity for the sake of activity. The USIA policy of decentralization assumes that the Public Affairs Officer knows best what is best for his area, and he has great latitude (subject, of course, to the approval of the ambassador). But in reality many Public Affairs Officers come from a background in journalism or radio and do not pretend to be able to evaluate events in the artistic and intellectual world, unless in terms of press coverage. On the other hand, many Cultural Affairs Officers feel the need for critical guidance, especially after several years overseas, and deplore the fact that they have to "be brilliant improvisers," as one officer put it. The advice should come, of course, from the most competent intellectual and artistic leadership in the United States.

The complexities of the task abroad

If discontent at home is not lacking, there is a good deal of evidence from overseas that the prestige of American thought and culture—and hence of its capacity for leadership—has actually been lower in the last few years than it was fifteen years ago. A recent anthology of current opinions, *As Others See Us: The United States through Foreign Eyes* (1959) contains a barrage of indictments from all over the world, reported by spokesmen who were evidently selected because of their known sympathy toward and long experience in the United States. It would be dreary to quote extensively from this chorus of jeremiads, which are often boring in their lack of freshness and originality, but a few comments are illuminating. A typical comment comes from South Africa: "Do not go to America. Everything is painless, effortless and brainless. The children are intolerable and the grown-ups, one cannot say 'adults,' scarcely less so. . . . There is no leadership in taste or politics." Some of the writers try to identify the sources of these derogatory views about United States policy and culture, and a number of them note the influence of European intellectuals. "Indian intellectuals," writes A. D. Gorwala, "find their views confirmed and strengthened by sources they have been accustomed to treat with respect; upper-class British opinion is particularly effective in this connection."

The case of Spain is particularly interesting, according to the philosopher Julian Marias, because the "current of aversion and hostility toward the United States" has become noteworthy only in the last few years, i.e. since Spaniards have begun to travel extensively in Europe, and to read more European books, newspapers and magazines. In fact, throughout this symposium—as in others that preceded it—the American reader is repeatedly struck by the extent to which spokesmen for the less powerful nations report that their views originated with or have been confirmed by European intellectuals, especially in France but often in Great Britain. These spokesmen may be hostile toward the colonial powers in fundamental ways, but in the realm of humanistic and artistic values there is no objection to intellectual colonialism, rather the contrary. To be sure, European writers like Raymond Aron have been issuing warnings about this for some time: his brilliant study of *The Opium of the Intellectuals* told us long ago that "Whether one likes it or dislikes it, welcomes or deplores it, the fact remains that the 'clerks' of Paris still play a role in the world and radiate an influence out of proportion to the place that France occupies on the map."

It is beyond the scope of this paper to attempt an analysis of the ingenious and sophisticated ramifications of French intellectual preconceptions about the United States, but perhaps an example is relevant. It is still a fairly general practice of French publishers, notably the powerful Gallimard, to reserve the acknowledgment *traduit de l'américain* in translated works for thrillers and other sensational and ephemeral paperbacks in the tawdry *série noire*. The standard expression used for serious writers of fiction, from Melville to Saul Bellow, is *traduit de l'anglais*. In an article in *Encounter* (Dec. 1961) the British critic Marcus Cunliffe has noted this curious fact and made the further discovery that a number of the "American translations" are actually the products of French authors who have thought up American-sounding pseudonyms whereby to promote these potboilers. Thus in a myriad of ways the "villainous image" of America is spread.

To be sure, the whole matter of the "image" of the United States among foreign intellectuals is an exceedingly complex one and has to be traced back in France well over a century. Recent collaborative studies by an American and a French scholar, Durand Echeverria and René

Remond, seem to prove that the last American who was really esteemed in France was Benjamin Franklin, and the last French writer who looked at the United States with fresh eyes was de Tocqueville—who incidentally is hardly known among French university students (it was the Rockefeller Foundation which prompted publication of a complete edition of his works, now finally slowly appearing).

To some extent the alleged permanent immaturity and violence of American culture is a French and European literary theme with a long lineage which may survive indefinitely. But along with the burden of the past which cannot be removed in any case, some friendly European observers feel that the United States has been exporting too much of the wrong kind of information about herself suddenly of late, after so many decades when the image was schematic and haphazard. "In recent times there has increasingly been too much information, often contradictory, of unequal reliability, from many sources," writes Julian Marias in a recent issue of *Foreign Affairs* (July 1961). But all this information and especially statistics—of which the United States compiles and exports a prodigious supply—in his view does not have the same meaning for foreigners because they start with quite different assumptions: "Unless there is a common assumption, language, instead of providing real communication, is misleading."

What is needed in order to bring the assumptions into closer alignment, according to Mr. Marias, is "background and perspective." It will not suffice to give "the last-minute developments in politics, the last week's economic data, the monthly progress in integration" in order to change the "image of the United States as an intellectual wasteland and of American writers, artists and thinkers as exiles in their own country which . . . is almost uncontested in European intellectual circles today."

In an earlier essay in the book *As Others See Us* this same observer explained more fully why he thinks misconceptions about the place of the artist and intellectual in American society are at the heart of anti-American prejudices:

. . . there is a dominant assumption in Europe today that "the American" represents only a modification, an amplification—many people would say a corruption—of "the European." Implied here is a lack of *originality* of the United States, an incapacity for *creation*. This in turn implies—and the assumption is widely held—monotony, vulgarity, "colossalism," intellectual inferiority. In certain respects the greatness of the United States is undeniable and is not denied, or at least infrequently. But this is understood to be merely a quantitative greatness and so suggests nothing really new or compelling. At most the United States is viewed as the country of the masses, where the superior individual has no role and rarely exists; the intellectual or the artist, be he American or foreign, is always an exile there, lost in a strange land of Philistines.

Obviously—as other friendly European critics note—the literary sources of these European assumptions are often native and the tradition of angry self-criticism from Mark Twain or Mencken to C. Wright Mills is long and articulate. But somehow there seems to be an insatiable appetite abroad for this particular fare. In part, as Aron and Cunliffe note, malice and envy enter the picture, along with communist propaganda. But still other factors are involved.

There is some evidence that the way our cultural exchange programs have been working has involuntarily served to foster the idea that the arts and the humanities have little place in American education and values. Robert Blum has noted that of the Asian students enrolled in American universities only about one-third are in the humanities and the social sciences; the majority specialize in engineering, medical, physical and natural sciences, agriculture, business administration and education. Although, in part, this reflects the shortage of technicians and specialists, there is also in play the Asian attitude toward American education, "which is often looked upon as being suitable in fields of practical study, but irrelevant or deficient where general ideas regarding society, history, philosophy, literature, and government are concerned. . . . This attitude was, and continues to be, nurtured by the British and French. . . . What is true of the Asian students is largely valid for the entire foreign student body: of nearly 50,000 foreign students in the United States in 1959-60, less than 10,000 were studying the humanities and the arts.

There appears to be a vicious circle. The majority of foreign students come to the United States with the preconception that artistic and humanistic values will not be found, and then they arrange their study programs so as to avoid any exposure to these fields, should they exist.

Meanwhile, what of the role of the creative artist in other exchange programs? Are mature American artists and creative persons being utilized to an extent that is commensurate with their actual role in American society? A recent Department of State report shows that 3,361 persons were involved in exchanges in the arts from 1952 through 1960, of a total of 57,757 grantees. Of these nearly half were American students (1,530) and another 25% (739) were foreign students. The total number of grants in all other categories was 1,092 (about 140 a year) including American and foreign lecturers, teachers, research scholars, specialists and leaders. This includes a high percentage of persons from the teaching profession—some of whom are primarily creative artists but many of whom are not.

The only non-academic government program which sends Americans overseas for cultural purposes other than teaching, study or research, is the American Specialists Program. Since 1949 when it started, about 230-240 Americans annually have received full or partial Smith-Mundt grants for overseas visits, usually for thirty to ninety days. As conceived originally, this would seem to be the ideal opportunity for creative persons;

and in fact a number of distinguished representatives have participated in it over the years—such writers as Katherine Anne Porter, William Faulkner, Allen Tate, Carl Sandburg and others. But in reality their visits have usually been fleeting, even in European countries. For years USIS cultural officers have been deploring the fact that so few distinguished lecturers and representatives came their way.

Many factors conspire to impede full utilization of the American Specialists Program in behalf of the artistic and intellectual community. In countries where there has been no Fulbright program, these Smith-Mundt funds have had to fill needs for teaching personnel, usually for periods much longer than ninety days, at high cost. In the last Olympic year, over twenty per cent of the grants were used to meet field requests for professional athletic coaches to train local participants in the Olympic games. In general, the American Specialists Program has been a catch-all for all the miscellaneous travel grants requested by overseas posts to carry out seminars, clinics, workshops, and exhibits in a variety of subjects ranging from plastics to puppetry. In commenting on this program Professor Laves recommends that there should be a highly qualified staff in Washington in a position to "develop a substantial reservoir of 'prestige' participants representing the top strata of American professional life," but the problem seems really to have lain with the administrative organization, which placed responsibility for planning with the field posts. A number of distinguished writers found that when they offered their services, it was difficult for government officials to reach a decision because the field posts had to be consulted. Fortunately the Fulbright-Hays Act provides for more rational operation of the Smith-Mundt grants, although it is not yet clear what mechanisms will be used for selecting grantees.

In recognition of the need for additional exchange opportunities in the cultural field, the number of foundation-sponsored grants in the arts and the humanities has been slowly growing in recent years. Since 1959 the Ford Foundation has supported the Institute of Contemporary Arts in Washington, which brings a number of artists, writers and other leaders to the United States annually. Another small Ford Foundation program administered by the Institute of International Education awards scholarships to foreign students in the arts. Ford Foundation fellowships for Americans under the International Training and Research Program also include a few in the creative arts: since 1952 there have been twenty-nine such fellows in art and architecture, twenty-one in music and two in dance. These opportunities supplement long-established, if also small, programs of the Rockefeller and Guggenheim Foundations, the Commonwealth Fund, the Harvard Summer Seminar and a few others.

It is true that these statistics do not take into account an indefinite number of cultural representatives who travel on their own initiative, with sabbatical leaves or private resources. And yet it is difficult to escape the conclusion that the total American effort has been modest and haphazard, especially compared with that of other governments. Statistics from the USSR may be inflated, but they suggest a different emphasis on these activities. "In the first eight months of 1959," we are told, "3,918 Soviet actors and other cultural workers went abroad (1,543 went to the Socialist countries), while 1,488 foreign actors and other cultural workers visited the Soviet Union (including 1,050 from the Socialist countries." *

The British Council also gives a high priority to what it calls "Specialist Tours, Advisory Visits and Delegations." "Our main task," wrote the Director-General recently in the 21st Anniversary Report, "is the making and fostering of contacts between individual people. We have not the resources, even if the attempt were desirable, to make any direct impact on the masses." Selection of individuals to go overseas is made by the various Advisory Committees and Panels which work closely with the Council staff in all activities.

The arts and area priorities

Ever since the beginning of United States government cultural exchange there has been a running debate as to whether these activities can or should conform to the objectives of foreign policy; and if so, whether to long- or short-range goals. In the case of the information programs, no such question exists. The fact that the two activities are merged overseas under the single administration of USIS has provided the appearance of a solution, or at least a truce, but a civil war has gone on steadily between those who seek immediate and spectacular success and those who believe cultural exchange should proceed quietly and steadily but with a few modest long-range ends hopefully in view.

But whichever position one takes—and in recent years partisans on both sides seem to have been about equally divided—neither point of view provides an automatic solution to the question of area priorities.

If this were an ideal world where it was unnecessary to think about politics, one might conclude that the universal language of the arts has a universal appeal and it is impossible to decide whether it matters more to the Japanese or the Brazilians or the Senegalese. In different ways, but with unanimous insistence, each area and country, with few exceptions, claims its own stake in the arts—and a need and a right to find self-expression and self-identity in its own writers and artists.

* Quoted by Oliver J. Caldwell, "What Others Are Doing," *Annals* of the American Academy of Political and Social Science, May 1961. The source is an article by Georgi A. Zhukov, "Two Approaches Towards Cultural Contacts," *International Affairs* (Moscow), No. 11 (November 1959).

Most people agree with Northrup that the civilization of East Asia can be characterized as aesthetic in contrast to the theoretic and logical approach of the West. Ambassador Reischauer in his many writings on Japan calls attention to the extent to which the arts—especially poetry and the graphic arts—have permeated Japanese life as a whole. For example: national poetry contests are not unusual, and even successful politicians are expected to be able to compose poems as well as speeches. Even in music, in which they had long lagged behind, the Japanese have recently shown the same kind of prowess in mastering the technique of playing the most difficult Western string instruments that marked their mastery of the refined art of Chinese prints in the nineteenth century. East Asia and especially Japan have many claims to very high area priority in cultural exchange.

In Latin America, where concern with cultural matters is restricted to a still small elite, the most informed observers warn that the political authority of these creative intellectuals cannot be overestimated. Salvador de Madariaga's views as expressed in the *Saturday Review* (March 25, 1961) are typical:

> In Latin America, however, a man may be writing poetry on Friday and become President or Minister of Foreign Affairs the following Sunday. Nor should one suppose that this phenomenon is limited to that form of power which derives from actual political functions. It cannot be doubted, for instance, that the high reputation which Pablo Neruda enjoys as a poet considerably enhances his power over Chilean public opinion as a Communist leader.
>
> No more grievous mistake could therefore be made by the public opinion of the United States than to shrug its shoulders at the pro-Soviet and anti-American wave that is sweeping intellectual circles in Latin America. From the ranks of these pink professors, poets, doctors, and lawyers, the men will be recruited who will actually govern Latin America not merely ten years hence, but maybe next year, maybe next month. The issue is immediate and urgent; and we must waste no time in facing it.

If one turns to the new countries of Africa, it is increasingly evident that in the thinking of their own leaders, cultural development is a primary and immediate need, for reasons both psychological and political. In the thinking of some of the most enlightened African leaders, the goal is not merely cultural development as a source of national identity and national pride, but also as a field in which regional cooperation can foster economic and political trends toward unification. However, it is not clear that the type of cultural assistance and development they need today can be supplied by routine USIS installations. For the past two years USIA has been rapidly opening large new posts in tropical Africa. This experiment does not seem to have the general approval of political officers in the area, who question the need for USIS staffs as large as those of the State Department. As one minister-counselor said recently, "I don't see what there is for a PAO or cultural officer to do, in a country where literacy is only five or ten per cent, and where the exchange programs are so tiny that we can run them. Rather than USIS officers, we need trained teachers and many other things first."

The cultural exchange program that the United States has with the countries of the Soviet bloc seems to be the most striking practical demonstration to date of the *political* usefulness of such contacts. Obviously it is too soon to draw far-reaching conclusions; and yet in the three brief years since the first exchange agreement went into effect a small handful of artists, humanists and scholars have managed to make the images the two peoples have of each other more complex, and perhaps it will be more difficult for the cold war to return in quite its former monolithic shape.

In view of the high priority of other areas, and the rapid increase in the number of countries, there has been a trend since 1956 toward ever sharper reduction of activities in Europe. By 1961 USIS posts in Western Europe had lost one-third of their American staff and nearly two-fifths of their local employees; the share of USIA funds expended in Western Europe had declined from about twenty to less than thirteen per cent. In 1962 a reduction of $550,000 caused the sharpest decrease to date in cultural (as well as information) activities; for 1963 a further ten per cent reduction was planned. Meanwhile, the diversion of resources from Europe affects not only the size of the effort but above all its quality. Since 1960 it has been USIA policy to assign many of its most mature and sophisticated officers to other priority areas, especially tropical Africa. With Europe thus "downgraded," it has followed inevitably that some of the most sensitive and challenging European assignments have fallen to persons who in no sense represent the best the United States (or the USIA) has to offer.

Recently a growing number of persons inside and outside the government have called attention to the need to focus attention again on Europe. *The New York Times* correspondent, C. L. Sulzberger, has more than once noted the extent of anti-Americanism in Europe, especially in Germany, and the resentment of what is often considered as a "patronizing" or "arrogant" attitude on our part (for example, *The New York Times,* August 8, 1962). But his apprehensions have long been anticipated by various USIA officers. In presenting the 1962 USIA budget to the House Appropriations Committee, the Assistant Area Director for Europe warned, months ago, that "events have shown that we cannot safely take those countries for granted."

It may be true—we do not know—that there is less need for government "information" programs in Europe than there was a few years ago. In matters that pertain to intellectual and cultural communication and understanding, our investigation has to conclude that the gulf between the old world and the new is still very deep. In fact, with the possible exception of Great Britain, anti-Americanism in the form of critical hostility toward American thought and culture has actually been increasing. In recent years it has been steadily promoted also by Soviet cultural diplomacy, which has given highest priority to Western Europe since 1951.

America as an idea

Whatever may be the state or status of our artistic and cultural resources, the United States has one asset not yet mentioned which demands attention: in spite of all, it still stands for an important idea—the idea that all men are created free and equal. It is an idea that is not only political but profoundly humanistic; a very simple idea, with universal appeal, whose implications are inexhaustible.

In its historical, strictly political context, the idea—and the very words —have served recently to inspire peoples, in Indonesia and Hungary, for example—in their struggles for national independence. But even where independence is achieved, it has to go on and illuminate the many other implications of what freedom means, and what makes for the dignity of individual human beings. This goes far beyond the question of political institutions and ideologies, and leads to the special domain of the artist —to the atelier where he is trying to create an image of man, working relentlessly to express his own ideals and those of other men. What he creates symbolizes things that are very difficult or impossible to say in words. While most people are concerned of necessity with institutions, governments, material things, abstract ideas, the artist is a reminder that all that matters in the end are individual persons.

This may seem far removed from the goals of foreign policy and yet an ultimate relationship is discernible, and indeed central. What we are trying to say has to do with the values stressed by Lloyd Free and Hadley Cantril in their study of United States international objectives quoted earlier:

> Ultimately, the kind of safe, defensible, friendly world we seek must be built upon people; upon individual human beings. Our habit of thinking in such abstract, impersonal terms as "political, economic and social revolutions," "assistance programs," "counterpart funds," "military alliances," "political, economic and social evolution," and the like, sometimes makes us forget that this is the basic reality with which we have to deal. The world is changing because people want it to change; it is evolving because human beings are on the march.
> The job required of us is to help them evolve as individual human beings,

not only economically, but politically, socially and psychologically. . . .

We should, in short, stop talking about "underdeveloped areas" and start thinking about "underdeveloped people." It is the gradual development of the human being which counts. He is no longer willing to stand still, but is ready and eager now to walk forward and upward. The problem is to help him get off his age-old treadmill and onto the long zigzag climb up the democratic mountain.

The role of the artists and writers in assisting this development of human beings—beyond what can and must be provided by economic, technical and educational aid—has to do with the other values that make individuals more human, freedom more meaningful, and life more complex.

Sometimes the artist or writer is the very personification of what we are trying to say without lapsing into sentimental or mystical platitudes. How this comes about is suggested by what happened recently in Poland when the American writers of the thirties and later were suddenly published en masse around 1956. As a young Polish critic explains in a recent issue of the *Kenyon Review* (Winter, 1961): "these books exploded many of the clichés and pat formulas by which the United States had always been judged; they were the proof of an unexpected diversity." The main reason why American writers were so admired was that they seemed to be so democratic and free: they "lead one from a literary salon into the fresh air. They write without deference to snobberies, conventions, or formulas . . . and they are careless about the social or political responsibilities of literature." Of all the writers who were tardily discovered in Poland in the mid-fifties, Hemingway was the most popular, and that happened because "Polish readers see Hemingway as a marvelous upholder of human liberty":

Hemingway is at home everywhere, in America, in Spain, and in Africa. Like his vagabond, soldier, traveler heroes, he is always on the move. Now, by making his hero someone who is always en route to another place, Hemingway is able to free him from all dependence on social mechanism, historical necessity—in fact from any kind of impersonal necessity. . . . [He introduces] the reader into a world where everything is possible, where the choice is up to us, and where—if we capitulate—we do not surrender because of any outside force but only because we lack the strength to conquer. . . .

Rightly or wrongly, Hemingway is taken as an optimist—is even taken as that rare animal, a great writer *and* great optimist.

Perhaps in the end it is the artist who communicates most clearly the good news that is implicit in the American idea.

Conclusions

In the introduction to this chapter, we argued that the most realistic and effective interchange among cultures and among artists would proceed without reference to foreign policy, and that even if public funds were used to assist such interchange this principle, ideally, should still prevail. But if broad political principles were needed to justify any activities by the United States government in these realms, it was said, then they should be kept broad and be at least generally related to the most basic philosophical assumptions underlying Western society, such as its ideal of man as an individual with paramount rights. It was doubted that without risk to their own peculiar values the arts could be employed for temporary and shifting objectives of national interest, such as increasing popular understanding of United States policies and institutions in particular regions of the world.

A corollary assumption is that art and cultural activities generally have a true importance for relatively small minorities in any society, even though these minorities contain those who cultivate and influence intellectual opinions and currents, and who thus have an importance beyond their numbers.

Our first two conclusions derive from this context: cultural exchange activities should not be confused with short-range "information" programs; and both legislative and administrative arrangements for government support of inter-cultural movements should permit longer range planning. (It should be noted that the Fulbright-Hays Act gave authority for appropriations to remain available until expended, and removed arbitrary ceilings on the annual size of country programs.) The implementation of these two conclusions would be greatly facilitated by acceptance of the third: the centralization of cultural affairs activities of the government in one office in Washington, and giving the cultural affairs officer abroad a status equal to that of the public affairs officer, through whom he now works in the normal USIS arrangement.

It is beyond the scope of this chapter to attempt to weigh all the arguments in Washington and in the field about the coordination and centralization of cultural activities being carried out by the State Department, USIA, AID, and other agencies. And yet it does appear that the role of cultural exchange within the present complex of USIA activities is a good deal more "muddy" and confused today than it was a few years ago. As a new and insecure Agency with ill-defined objectives, status and relationship to the Department of State and other government branches including the White House, USIA leadership seems to have tried to protect its role—essential indeed—by attempting constantly to be in the vanguard of the shifting spotlight on day-to-day crises in foreign policy.

Such flexibility and alertness is no doubt appropriate to the fast media of which USIA disposes—although there is a question whether even the fast media should be primarily responsive to very short-range issues.

But what seems beyond question is that a preoccupation with the immediate has no place in a serious cultural program. We would further say that the present hierarchy of values within USIA should be reversed, and the higher priority in planning, staffing and financing should go to the long-range cultural program. If such a prospect is altogether utopian and at variance with the present order of values in American society itself, then one has to conclude reluctantly that cultural activities should be administratively severed from USIA information activities, and placed either within the Department of State (where AID and the Peace Corps now are), or in a new independent office combining all the cultural programs now variously handled by USIA, the State Department, AID and others. In such an event, to be sure, USIA officers now serving in an information or public affairs capacity should have the opportunity to transfer without loss of rank to the cultural program, if their preparation and interest so qualify them.

In introducing this chapter, we said that the farther one moves from an ideal situation in which intercultural movements spontaneously manifest the vitality and the needs of the artists themselves, the more one needs to cling to strictly artistic considerations when he attempts to use the arts for other large purposes. We also argued the importance of ensuring for such activities the moral and intellectual support of the artistic community at home and abroad. Our fourth conclusion, therefore, is that no program of international cultural exchange, and no administrative system for executing it, can succeed without profiting at every turn from the intensive and realistic advice of artists and artistic directors themselves. This would seem to be obvious, but even so it has too often escaped the grasp of the State Department and USIA in Washington.

To the present date, neither the composition nor the use made of the Advisory Committee on the Arts has reflected artistic considerations or even an awareness of their importance. A small Music Advisory Panel in the USIA has been better used. Social, jurisdictional, even "logrolling" vagaries have characterized the employment of the American National Theatre and Academy as the operating instrument for the President's Cultural Presentations Program in the State Department. But worst of all has been the feeling among Washington officials responsible for cultural exchange that artists and artistic directors are by nature difficult, impractical, or mysterious in the role of consultants. The real problem is that few government officials have tried to learn what the arts and the artists are about. They bring to these fields the same vagueness of cultural and social generality that leads them to believe that the United

States *ought* to have a folk-dance company rivalling the Ukrainian, Polish, Philippine, or Ceylonese, even though there is not one indigenous or professional company among otherwise very large American artistic resources.

Anyone who has had experience in developing programs through the exclusive employment of artists and artistic directors as consultants, realizes that the government's greatest weakness in its intercultural activities has been the absence of practical, moral, and intellectual support by those persons who understand artistic enterprises. It is also a tribute to the shortsightedness of Congressional committees and certain top government officials that the manner in which the government entered the arts on the international scene has *a priori* convinced a majority of professionals in the arts that the United States should stay out of the field at home.

Reorganization and reorientation of the government's administration of cultural exchange are also involved in our fifth conclusion: governments, even more than private foundations, must act with extreme care when trying to use non-American local organizations for cultural activities that professedly are related to American foreign policy. In the mid-fifties, officials in Washington, by agreeing to strong decentralization of authority to public affairs officers in the field, in effect let their own proper control go by default. At times important amounts of local operating currencies of USIS have been tied up in recurring grants to activities managed by others than Americans and sometimes actually anti-American in propaganda, either consciously and subtly or through sheer ignorance about United States policies.

The warning that the government should not without the greatest care act as a regranting agency to local agencies of control may be particularly timely in view of the new mechanisms theoretically made available by the Fulbright-Hays legislation. Conceivably the entire USIS cultural program overseas might now be administered through the device of the binational commission. But experience with such commissions where they have already been employed has often proved that their assumptions about the United States and what it has to offer in the cultural field were far removed from realities.

Multilateral arrangements, it is agreed, should be more frequently employed in cases where the United States shares a common purpose with other highly-developed countries. This is especially relevant with regard to multilateral arrangements with Western European countries, and within that sector with particular reference to cultural activities to be carried out in the newly developing nations.

Our broadest conclusion, of course, must go to the question of the worth, actual and potential, of United States international cultural activities. It is clear from the text that in the opinion of the authors, we should have to judge these activities not to have been an imporant category of United States expenditures if we used only the yardstick of a "better image" of America abroad. It is clear, however, that we are not in sympathy with judging international exchange from the point of view either of competition with the Soviets or of short-term improvements in foreign understanding of American policies. In our opinion, the reduction of our activities in Europe to the advantages of activities elsewhere was not based upon assumptions that were valid *either* for intercultural objectives or for foreign policy considerations. Our final conclusion is that our international cultural activities should be expanded, and primarily in Western Europe.

Since 1950, despite the careful observations of some of our representatives in Europe who had the most deeply rooted cultural contacts there, we have had the illusion that we and the Europeans saw eye to eye because all our governments were lined up solidly against the Soviet Union. Now as American foreign policy leaders explore some new design for "the Atlantic Community," we all need to explore three myths that have been taken for granted since about 1948—the myth about European colonialism, the myth about European understanding of Americans through an historical sharing of common values, and the myth that "information" programs can be trusted to relate Americans and Europeans toward common values.

The myth about colonialism has led to the theory that we should disassociate ourselves as much as possible from the European colonial powers and deal only directly with the new and emerging nations. But now we are beginning to see that the new nations, once they are free, are still in need of Europe and in fact wish to import many of their ideas and values from her, including their evaluation of United States culture. For this and other reasons, we have to work with Europe now, facing the problems not only of an Atlantic community but of relating this community to the so-called "underdeveloped" parts of the world.

That the Europeans automatically share our values and understand us is a myth tardily being exploded as we face that day-to-day problems of working with them outside the purely military context of NATO (and sometimes, even within that context). Some Americans stationed in Europe have known this for years, but their long battle to convince us was frustrated both by the complacency of many of their local colleagues and by the desire of administrators and legislators in Washington to hear only about success and novelty.

Related to this complacency about the solidarity of the Atlantic Community is the naive idea it can be kept up to date by international programs that concentrate on "news" and "information." It may be necessary, in order to change the mentality, to abandon the name "United States *Information* Agency," even if the recommendations made above for taking cultural activities out of the USIA should become necessary and be adopted.

If the arts and the humanities are of any use at all to the government's objectives, they are of use only to those of the longest range and concerned with the most basic intellectual and cultural currents running among peoples of varying political and economic origins. The assumptions that underlie the international objectives we share with Western Europe have to do with the values people live by. And here the arts and the humanities, if not distorted from their own realities, have a role to play.

Howard E. Wilson

3

Education, Foreign Policy, and International Relations

When the Covenant of the League of Nations was drafted in 1919 it contained no reference to educational relations among nations, but when the Charter of the United Nations was adopted in 1945 it provided for a Specialized Agency devoted to education, science, and culture. These two facts span a characteristic development of the twentieth century—the recognition of education as a factor in the foreign policy of modern states, an ingredient in the complex pattern of international relations.

Exchange of educational ideas, policies and practices among nations is, of course, a time-honored process. The United States, for example, borrowed heavily from German patterns in developing American universities during the nineteenth century, and more recently has been influenced by Scandinavian practices in adult education. Our own distinctive patterns of the comprehensive high school, of counseling practices, of junior colleges have been widely copied abroad in recent years. French practices in secondary education have influenced large areas of the world; the word

---

HOWARD E. WILSON *is dean of the School of Education at U.C.L.A. and Professor in the field of Comparative Education. While on the faculty of the Harvard Graduate School of Education (1928-1945), Dr. Wilson was editor of the* Harvard Educational Review, *president of the National Council for the Social Studies, and director of research projects for the American Council on Education. From 1945 to 1953, he was Executive Assistant in charge of the education programs of the Carnegie Endowment; and from 1953 to 1957 was Secretary of the Educational Policies Commission. He served as Deputy Executive Secretary of the Unesco Preparatory Commission in 1946. In 1959 he was consultant to a Turkish national commission on education.*

lycée is now at home in many languages. Contemporary Turkey is sometimes described as having American elementary schools, French secondary schools, and German universities. The educational philosophers of all the centuries are read in every land.

In the past, the exchange of educational ideas and the emulation of foreign models has been a natural process largely unaffected by political and nationalistic considerations or by governmental operations. But to this historical process, slow-moving and directed often by chance, something new has been added in the present century. For one thing, education became a factor in the governance of colonial empires. The British developed an imperial and subsequently a commonwealth policy of education which facilitated both economic and civic development among vast numbers of people. Wherever the French flag went, French schools followed. One of the major legacies of the United States in the Philippines was a school system patterned after that of the United States. The Soviet Union tightened its grip on satellite areas by control of education. After World War II, as never before, educational rehabilitation in war-damaged territories became a matter of international, governmental policy and action. And educational reform by the occupying powers in such areas as Germany and Japan became postwar reconstruction.

EDUCATION AS A PART OF FOREIGN POLICY

While imperial politics, dictatorial techniques, humanitarian impulses, and postwar reconstruction all accented the role of education in international affairs, a deeper movement was under way. Education was becoming a conscious part of foreign policy, an instrument of international relations utilized by all modern states. France set a pattern for this early in the century by creating an education unit within its Ministry of Foreign Affairs—a unit devoted to increasing French prestige and influence by extending French culture. French schools were founded abroad; distinguished lecturers were sent to foreign universities; French books and works of art were widely distributed. Great Britain, two decades later, created the British Council as a semi-autonomous, publicly financed agency to establish libraries of British publications in leading cities of Asia and Europe and Africa, to promote English as a second language, and to provide scholarships for foreign students coming to Britain.

Developments in the United States

In the United States, the Division of Cultural Affairs in the Department of State—which began in 1938 with one policy officer and one full-time secretary—has now grown into a full Bureau of Educational and Cultural Affairs, headed, since 1961, by an Assistant Secretary of State. Before the Second World War, its operations were limited largely to the Western Hemisphere, but were greatly proliferated during the war, and have increased enormously since 1945. In August, 1946, the imaginative legislation proposed by Senator Fulbright as an amendment to the War Surplus Property Act was enacted. It has since made the term Fulbright synonymous with a scholarly exchange fellowship, has become a permanent part of American governmental action, has affected an increasing number of countries, and has provided "Fulbrighters" on almost every campus in the United States. In 1948, the Smith-Mundt Act authorized a cultural relations program and an information service on a world-wide basis. Under its authority the United States Information Service and the Office of Educational Exchange were established.

So varied and complex had the governmental activities in this field become by 1961, that a codification of them became necessary and was effected in the Fulbright-Hays Act. The Act regularizes a vast program of cultural relations, provides for coordination through the Department of State's Bureau of Educational and Cultural Affairs, interrelates governmental and non-governmental responsibilities and programs. The Fulbright-Hays Act marks the end of what Philip H. Coombs, the first person appointed Assistant Secretary of State for Educational and Cultural Affairs, has referred to as the "freshman period" of American operations in this field. In effect, a new relationship between education, foreign policy, and international relations has been brought about. It did not occur easily or without controversy. In the United States, as in every other country, education and propaganda have been frequently confused. Occasional enthusiasts have forgotten that, in the end, education is a matter of domestic concern to every nation, that educational relations among nations must be cooperatively developed rather than imposed by one on the other. But the general movement of the last six decades toward governmental use of education in a far-sighted foreign policy is clear and unmistakable. Educational relations among states are a part of the total diplomatic action which is a bulwark against total war.

FUNCTIONS OF EDUCATION IN INTERNATIONAL AFFAIRS

One of the complicating factors in assessing education's role in contemporary international relations is the confused mixture of functions that education is expected to play in a nation's foreign policy. Different people see different motivations in the same educational operations, and it is only as motives and functions are clarified that evaluation and long-range planning can take place.

In general it can be argued that the role of education in foreign policy is important because it is in the interest of the United States. But the very statement supposes a long-range point of view toward the national interest. It is of no immediate value to us that American practices and concepts of education be copied abroad, except as education in those countries contributes to economic advancement, political stability, and cultural vitality as it does in the United States. We gain nothing, except perhaps the satisfaction of an empty pride, by transplanting junior colleges, or comprehensive high schools, or land-grant universities, or student counseling programs abroad, except as these distinctively American developments serve significant and satisfying purposes in their new cultural setting. Indeed, it may well be argued that superficial transplantations incapable of taking root in the new cultures are in the end harmful to all concerned.

The pragmatic tradition of American education has particular value in newly developing cultures. This tradition is not a mere emphasis on vocationalism, but is rather a conviction that education is applicable to the solution of the problems of existence—that learning and life are indistinguishable, that there is no wide gap between school and society. It brings technology and the humanities into a framework of general education, and assumes that education is a crucial factor in economic and political welfare. Education is not only for an elite, fortunately able to escape the drudgeries of living, but for everybody, and useful in living. It is this complex of ideas and assumptions that makes United States education a desired quality, particularly in the less developed areas of the world. To the degree that it is desired, the American experience in education is a legitimate export, useful to the United States in its international relations.

Education-for-development, then, is inevitably a factor of consequence in United States foreign policy. As development aid has been stressed through technical assistance programs, culminating thus far in the work of the Agency for International Development (AID), education has become more important as an instrument in foreign aid. As technical assistance has moved into "institution building" and into the cultivation of trained manpower, educational programs have expanded in all the less developed areas in which the United States is active. In this respect, the function of education in foreign policy is national development in less advanced areas. Its goal is to help establish economic prosperity within free societies—the basic goal of all foreign aid programs of the United States.

But there are objectives in the use of education in foreign policy which rise beyond self-interest or national interest. To provide equality of educational opportunity for all is a part of the American dream. Advance through education is a part of the universal hope of mankind. In an article in the June, 1962, *International Development Review,* Fowler

Hamilton, Director of AID, writes of seeing a little girl in Hongkong learning arithmetic while seated beside her mother who was working at the oars of a boat. In Nigeria recently, the principal of a new secondary school learned that the boy working the outboard motor on a dugout canoe used as a river ferry had spent his first earned money to pay the fee for taking admission examinations to enter the school. These are satisfying experiences. Every Peace Corps teacher feels an upward lift when he enables a student to learn. Making education available to larger and larger numbers of people is an objective in itself—one of the values we cherish, made all the more consequential by America's inescapable responsibilities of world power. Americans want everyone to have access to an education almost as a birthright. A foreign policy which furthers that desire is satisfying to many American citizens and appealing in many areas of the world.

What has thus far been said about the functions of education in foreign policy is primarily applicable to areas undergoing rapid development—to our relations with new nations which are trying to telescope centuries into decades. But there is another function, both altruistic and in the national interest, which applies heavily to our relations with the more advanced nations of the world. Learning is itself universal. The devotion to any branch of learning to which a scholar commits himself requires communication with his colleagues elsewhere. To advance learning through research by facilitating the exchange of scholars, by maintaining open channels of communication, by aiding advanced students sent to or received from all the world is a legitimate and even essential function of the modern state. It is this function which the Fulbright grants have served. As the advance of learning becomes less and less provincial, this function of education in foreign policy demands increased attention. A technological democracy must be on the cutting edge of intellectual and aesthetic advancement, and for this a widening network of international relations is essential.

EXCHANGE OF PERSONS

By all odds, the most general and continuous procedure in international educational relations is the exchange of persons who are concerned with education and attached to educational institutions. Students and scholars, since the foundation of the earliest universities, have moved about among centers of learning. Within the twentieth century, student movement has been organized and regulated and expanded as never before. Special student visas have been developed, bursaries and scholarships established, equivalence of academic standards analyzed. Large-scale programs both for sending and receiving students have been established by governments, although the major volume of student exchange is still privately financed. More students and scholars now study or teach or carry on research outside their homeland for periods of time than in any preceding era of history. These exchanges are in some ways more restricted and regulated now than formerly, and are more intimately related to national policies and to the issues of international action than ever before.

Foreign students in the United States

Although the records are not very exact, it is estimated that, in 1930, the United States was host to just under 10,000 foreign students. By 1962, according to the census reported by the Institute of International Education in its annual publication, *Open Doors,* there were 58,086 students from 149 countries or areas studying in 1,798 United States institutions of higher education. The number of these students has been increasing about 7 per cent a year for the last decade. If this rate of increase should continue, the United States would receive almost 132,000 foreign students in 1970.

A fourth of the students now coming are registered in the colleges and universities of three states—California, New York, and Michigan—but students are now more widely distributed among all the states and all types of educational institutions than ever before. Seventeen American universities register more than 500 foreign students each; 9 of the 17 are publicly supported institutions. In only 9 of our universities do foreign students account for as much as 5 per cent of the total student group. Howard University with 16.1 per cent of its students from outside the United States and Massachusetts Institute of Technology with 12.3 per cent are unusual in this respect. On most American campuses less than one per cent of the student population is foreign. About 30 per cent of all foreign students in the United States are self-supporting; the United States government grants funds to about 9 per cent of the total; foreign government grants, and foundation and other private funds contribute to the others. Slightly more than half the total group in 1962 were undergraduates. The students come from every area of the world—37 per cent of them from the Far East, 17 per cent from Latin America, 14 per cent from the Near and Middle East, 12 per cent from Europe, 11 per cent from Canada and Mexico; 7 per cent from Africa. A total of 59 students came from the U.S.S.R. As to fields of study—22 per cent were in engineering, 19 per cent in the humanities, 16 per cent in the natural and physical sciences, 14 per cent in the social sciences. Others, in diminishing numbers, were students in business administration, medicine, education, and agriculture.

There has been a good deal of wishful thinking, both in the colleges and in the government, about these foreign students. In the early post-war years, particularly, the necessity for providing a good education was seriously compromised by the desire to win friends for America. Too frequently, colleges received foreign students in a gesture of friendship, and modified standards of achievement to meet the circumstances. Some students returned home with memories of a happy sojourn but without very much in the way of effective education. Others were baffled by the adjustments to a different cultural milieu, irritated by collegiate restrictions or by the "red tape" of visa and other requirements. While most students seem to have profited by their American visit, the results are not always advantageous for the individual student or conducive to friendship for America. In the last decade, however, there have been marked improvements in the selection and reception of foreign students, in counseling them on academic matters, in adjusting them to American living, and in adherence to academic standards in estimating their achievement. Few universities are now without a foreign-student adviser, who is professional in his approach to his tasks.

At the same time, certain basic policy questions about foreign students must be faced in the United States. Should we receive these students in increasing numbers during the coming decade, when the population bulge in the United States will place unprecedented burdens on higher education? As will be indicated later, the United States receives about a quarter of all the students in the world studying outside their own country. Even so, these students constitute a smaller proportion of our total student body than do the foreign students of a number of other nations. The United States produces about a third of the college students of the world. Should we admit a third of those who study outside their own country? These over-all figures point up a problem but do not answer it. The answer lies in what is the responsibility of the United States and in what advantages may accrue from receiving foreign students. In terms of responsibility, we cannot escape heavy involvements in the education of free men. To reduce the flow of students to this country would have serious repercussions abroad. And it would also have serious effects on American higher education. Foreign students on American campuses are a resource of great strength in the education of Americans about the world in which they live. They have enriched the learning and widened the horizons of their American hosts. We should then, on educational as well as national policy grounds, continue to receive large numbers of students from abroad. The figure, earlier mentioned, of 132,000 such students by 1970 does not seem unwarranted.

It may and should be asked, now and later, whether we are receiving the foreign students we should be serving. It is by no means likely that we can provide academic places for all who seek admission. We have, in the past, admitted numbers of foreign students not adequately prepared to undertake the collegiate programs for which they came. In more recent years, we have tended to be more exacting; this policy should be pursued even further, both to avoid frustration in students not able to succeed and in order to make sure that the foreign graduates of American education are among the ablest of their countrymen. Recognizing fully the varieties of pre-college education found in different cultures, American colleges and universities should make certain that applicants for admission are in the upper percentiles of ability within the groups from which they come. For the very able, financial help should be available; admission of foreign students should not hinge upon financial status. To admit the less able, though it be humane, is to risk the frustrations of personal failure and to weaken United States prestige in the competition among nationals trained in different societies. In the context of the cold war, it is more advantageous for the United States to be represented by able returnees than by less able former students. The standards for admission and achievement in American colleges and universities are likely to become more rigorous in the coming decade, and must be made so for foreign as well as for American students. Selective recruitment of particularly talented young men and women should be a basic principle in American reception of foreign students and should be adhered to rigorously as the population pressures for place in higher education become greater.

We should take every precaution to keep the doors of opportunity wide open to the politically uncommitted youth of the world. To exclude students who have not already committed themselves to the West is to miss an opportunity of influencing the uncommitted group. Political as well as economic barriers to study in America should be kept at the lowest level possible. In the recruitment and selection of candidates—crucial to the success of programs of foreign study!—it is probable that American embassies abroad should play a stronger professional and supporting role than they now do. Individual colleges and universities cannot do adequate screening abroad—and cannot easily and humanely screen rigorously after candidates have arrived in the United States. Regional offices on a continental basis, now provided by the Institute of International Education, are helpful but not sufficiently local to be efficient. In a number of cases, groups of American institutions can send screening committees abroad in connection with particular programs—as in the case of the consortium of universities which is now selecting students from Africa, or of the National Association of Junior Colleges which sent a selection agent into the same area. In the end, it may be more continuously efficient to provide in embassies all over the world, cultural or educational attaches who are equipped to select students on a professional basis and to evaluate prospective students in terms of criteria supplied by the colleges themselves. In this area, there should be explored the possibility of increasingly close collaboration between the regional offices of the Institute of International Education, the cultural offices of embassies within their areas, and the admissions offices of American universities.

A good deal of thought has been given to the question of what educational level is best for a student's sojourn abroad. There is evidence that those who come for a year in an American high school, as under the exchange programs of the American Field Service, become deeply committed to American life. Living in American homes and being ordinarily lionized in the schools they attend, they become definitely Americanized. Returning home to continue their advanced studies, they later make the transition from schooling to career with minimum difficulty, while retaining a somewhat nostalgic affection for their American experience. College level students who are here for four years may also be quite Americanized, but the necessary adjustments for entering on a career directly after returning home are frequently difficult and are often attached psychologically to the American experience. Students from countries comparable in cultural pattern to the United States who stay here for one or two college years—an experience comparable to that of Americans who spend a junior year abroad—ordinarily have only minor adjustment problems either here or on their return home. For all these younger foreign students the American visit may be a deeply influential cultural experience. Graduate students are ordinarily more concerned with academic matters than with this cultural experience, significant as the latter is. Arriving usually with a more thorough educational grounding in their own culture, and committed to more definite career objectives at home, they tend to avoid the extremes of cultural alienation or identification with America. Moreover, their career plans are likely to be more definite and more realistic, and the vocational frustrations of returning home are less severe.

At present we receive very few high school students, very many college students, and a growing group of graduate students. Such United States grants as the Fulbright awards are largely focused on graduate and postgraduate levels. This policy seems to be wise and should be continued. During coming years the proportion of high school students coming may well be increased, though predominantly under private financial support. The proportion of college students should probably decline—though the actual numbers will increase—while the major growth should be encouraged at the graduate level. It is at this level that American higher education can make its most distinctive contribution, both to the advancement of learning and to the role of education in American foreign policy.

In this connection, however, it should be observed that American junior colleges may well receive substantially larger proportions of foreign undergraduates and enrollees in special programs than in the past. In many junior colleges this will call for the development of policies and student services which do not now exist. It may well require more careful explanation abroad of the distinctive role of junior colleges in the American system. The junior college may provide two-year terminal courses of a technical nature which are particularly appropriate for students from developing countries, as well as provide an introductory orientation for university-bound students. These possibilities are under study by a special committee of the National Association of Junior Colleges and are likely to be of increasing importance in the coming decade.

The length of time spent in study abroad is a factor of some consequence. The university centers of Europe have attracted for many decades students from other continents, no few of whom become permanent expatriates. London and Paris have today their share of "perpetual students"—as does the United States. There is a particular tendency for students who, for reasons of political change at home, cannot return to continue their student status indefinitely. In general, however, the United States has tended to limit the stay of foreign students, both under the terms of student visas and by making grants for limited periods only. The period of time which is best for a given student cannot, however, be established by a general arbitrary rule. It is desirable for each student's stay to be regulated by the academic purpose for which he is admitted. The length of time required for securing a given degree, or for completing a research assignment, or for completing a known program of study is the basic criterion for length of stay. For all foreign students there should be a periodic evaluation of progress toward a goal, participated in by the institutional foreign adviser, the appropriate governmental agency, and the student-sponsoring agency.

It must be concluded that the reception and education of foreign students is of great importance to many persons and nations abroad, to American educational institutions, to the advancement of learning, and to the kind of world toward which American foreign policy is directed. The number of foreign students is likely to increase. Much has been learned about the selection and handling of foreign students, but much more remains to be learned. Selective recruitment of outstandingly able students, careful development of their programs in terms of their needs, and with emphasis on academic purposes should guide future policy.

United States students abroad

Much that has been said about foreign students in the United States can also be said about Americans who become foreign students abroad. The Institute of International Education, in its most recent edition of *Open Doors* reports that 19,836 United States students were enrolled in 590 institutions located in 66 foreign countries in the 1960-1961 academic year. This was an increase of 30 per cent over the number registered in the preceding year. Ninety-four per cent of this number, however, were in 15 host countries. Mexico (3,717), France (2,906), Canada (2,241), United Kingdom (1,701), Germany (1,542), Austria (1,116), Switzerland (1,073), and Vatican City (1,061); each received more than a thousand American students in 1960-1961. Of the total group, 61 per cent were in Europe, 19 per cent in Latin America, 11 per cent in Canada, and 5 per cent in the Far East. Many of these were abroad for a single year under some form of the Junior Year Abroad. Many were there under American tutelage, residing on off-campus centers of their American university, or in such United States-type institutions as Mexico City College. In the summer the numbers given here were greatly increased by a variety of study-tours, many excellent and serious, some relatively touristic.

Most of the American undergraduates going abroad for a period of study were privately financed or sponsored by American institutions or non-governmental organizations. At the graduate level the situation was somewhat different. While some students were undertaking advanced studies on their own initiative and with their own funds, many were recipients of such aid as the Rhodes Scholarships, divers foundation grants, and, occasionally, travel fellowships of their own universities. A considerable proportion of Americans doing graduate study abroad received government aid through some such program as the Fulbright plan. Graduate students were more academically focused in their work abroad; they were scattered more widely over the world than the undergraduate group; and they were accumulating in their research studies information and insight more directly contributory to knowledge and learning in the United States. Whether engaged in historical and literary work in Western Europe, or on languages in Africa and Asia, on anthropological studies among relatively primitive groups, on research in medicine and public health, on geographic or political or economic or educational studies, their sojourns abroad had pertinence to the advancement of American scholarship, often in matters significant for an enlightened foreign policy.

It is probable that the number and range of graduate fellowships, particularly for research in connection with dissertations, should be substantially increased. Public funds invested in such programs on a larger scale than at present would be a wise investment contributory to the enhancement of learning in America and the rest of the world. Such programs should not be dependent so much upon registration and formal study in a foreign university, but should also be concerned largely with individual research, often field research. The experience of the Fulbright awards to graduate students affords ample evidence of the desirability of increased federal appropriations for this purpose. It is at the graduate student level that a major drive for the training of young scholars, for the accumulation of far-scattered information through their researches, and for the cultivation of a sophisticated outlook on world relations can be most rewarding.

Exchange of teachers

One program of exchange which has not received great publicity is that of direct interchange of teachers. Administered for the Department of State by the United States Office of Education, the program has effected an interchange of 2,277 American teachers with counterparts abroad since 1946, has sent 1,182 American teachers to one-year teaching posts abroad, and has brought 240 foreign teachers for a year of experience in the United States. One hundred American teachers exchange positions with 100 teachers in the United Kingdom each year; smaller interchanges are arranged annually with Australia, Austria, Belgium, Canada, Chile, France, Germany, Italy, Luxembourg, the Netherlands, New Zealand, Norway, and Peru. Under the ordinary terms of these interchanges, each teacher receives his home salary together with a government stipend covering travel costs, and, in some cases, a cost-of-living adjustment. One-way assignments for teachers operate in a larger number of countries, stress the teaching of English, and often involve service in an American elementary and secondary school abroad.

This program, carefully administered, has been outstandingly successful. It has provided something in the nature of an internship in comparative education for teachers, and has contributed both to the cultural outlook and the professional competence of the persons involved. It is strongly recommended that local school systems throughout the United States take more advantage of the possibilities in the program, and that local school boards make what alterations are necessary in regulations concerning reception of foreign teachers and ensurance of tenure, promotion, and retirement benefits for participating teachers. While the program operates most easily between countries with a common language and relatively well developed school systems, it may be advantageously extended to other areas, including less developed nations. It is a good investment for teachers and their regular employers, and for the mutual understanding of the nations involved.

Exchange of professors and research scholars

In governmental operations under the Fulbright and Smith-Mundt Acts major emphasis has been given to exchange of persons at the advanced levels of scholarship and research. For example, in 1961-1962, 5,530 scholars from 90 countries were affiliated with 390 colleges and universities in 48 of the states, the District of Columbia, and Puerto Rico. This was a radical increase over the number of such visitors during the previous year. Forty-one per cent of these visiting scholars were from Europe, 34 per cent from the Far East, 9 per cent from Latin America,

7 per cent from the Near and Middle East, and 4 per cent from Canada. The small number of visiting professors from Africa (119) nevertheless represented an increase of 58 per cent over the previous year. Japan, the United Kingdom, India, and Germany contributed almost half of the total. By all odds, the largest number of these scholars were in the scientific fields, including medicine. Only 715 of the total of 5,530 were in the humanities, and 497 in the social sciences.

During the same academic year, *Open Doors* reports that 2,427 American faculty members were on educational assignments in 90 countries. The ten countries receiving the largest number, in order, were the United Kingdom, Italy, France, Germany, India, Pakistan, Nigeria, Japan, Brazil, and Indonesia. Most of the visiting faculty members come from the humanities, with social sciences second, and the natural and physical sciences third—a direct reversal of the fields of imported scholars.

Post doctoral exchanges have had major attention by the United States government. These exchanges have, for the most part, been highly advantageous. They have added to American faculties many able visitors, and have further enriched the American academia by providing its regular faculty members periods of assignment abroad. Hardly an American campus is without a returned Fulbrighter or a Fulbright visitor from abroad. This operation, by all objective considerations, has been one of the finest cultural enterprises undertaken by government, with every participating person and nation enriched by the experience. It is a governmental operation in the tradition of the best of the private foundations—a legitimate public responsibility earlier validated by non-governmental programs in the names of Carnegie, Rockefeller, Guggenheim, and Ford.

Fulbright awards are given on the initiative and promise of individual applicants, endorsed by their employing institutions, and screened through a series of committees. There should be more planned assignment of awards on the basis of the cultural and educational needs of the United States, and the needs and policies of individual colleges and universities. If, for example, an institution is planning for expansion in its sociology program, it could advantageously take the initiative in selecting young sociologists as nominees for awards. The university should take the initiative in recruiting nominees in its institutional interest as seriously as an individual candidate takes the initiative in his own behalf. And, by the same token, at the national level greater attention should be given to awards in areas of scholarship which are of general American cultural concern. If, to use an example from the field of education, we are nationally concerned with better education for the particularly gifted, Fulbright awards in education might systematically be used to bring to us studies on the experience of other countries in this matter.

Exchanges in other countries

The United States is not unique in its reception of foreign students and scholars or its dispatch of our own students and scholars for sojourns abroad. As was indicated earlier, France, Great Britain, and Germany have had long experience in this field, and the U.S.S.R. is now heavily engaged in enterprises of this character. Many smaller states also seek foreign academic visitors—Yugoslavia, for example, finances several hundred students from abroad each year. Fellowships and awards for traveling students and scholars are provided by most modern states as well as by foundations and other private agencies.

UNESCO has rendered a unique service by preparing annually since 1948 a register of the scholarships, fellowships, and other awards available for study outside one's own country. The latest directory, called *Study Abroad*, contains information on more than 115,000 individual opportunities for international study offered in 1962 by more than 1,674 awarding agencies in 115 states and territories. About 16 per cent were granted by international agencies, 48 per cent by governments, 6 per cent by foundations, 20 per cent by educational institutions, and 10 per cent by other agencies. The number of these awards has increased annually; it increased by 15,000 in the interval between the 1961 and 1962 reports by UNESCO. Many more awards are available for foreigners to come to a donating country than for citizens of that country to be sent abroad—a reflection, doubtless, not only of humanitarian motives, but also of the pressures and competitions of the cold war. The UNESCO report indicates that most of the awards are in the applied sciences, followed, in order, by those in the social sciences (including education), natural science and mathematics, and the humanities.

In recent years UNESCO has gathered data concerning the total body of foreign students in institutions of higher education throughout the world. The latest report available, giving figures for the academic year 1958-1959, indicates that about 200,000 students were studying at the college or university level outside their homelands. This group comprised about 2 per cent of the world's total number of university students of that year, estimated at 11.5 million persons.

UNESCO reports in *Study Abroad:*

About one quarter of the foreign students were enrolled in institutions of higher education in the United States of America; yet the percentage of foreign students in relation to the total enrolled in that country is less than the world average. After the United States come the Federal Republic of Germany, France, the United Kingdom, and the U.S.S.R., each of which receives more than 10,000 foreign students. Argentina might be added to this group, for in 1957 it had 9,267 foreign students in its institutions of higher education.

It is obvious that interchange of academic personnel is an important and growing aspect of twentieth-century life, and that the United States is heavily involved in it. It is probable that the number of foreign students and scholars seeking admission to the United States will increase steadily, and it is to be hoped that places can be provided for those who are academically admissible to the programs they seek to undertake. It is also probable that we should send abroad larger numbers of United States academic citizens, particularly at the advanced graduate level, and that these students and scholars, carrying on appropriate research and field study, should be far less concentrated in Europe than is now the case.

EDUCATION AND NATIONAL DEVELOPMENT

Exchange of students and scholars is carried on, in some degree, with countries all over the world—the established and mature nations and those that are currently emerging into statehood, including industrialized and non-industrialized societies, large and small states, and highly varied cultures, races, and religions. The human talent and aspiration on which this educative interchange rests know no national boundary lines. But a second major area of United States educational activity, obviously overlapping extensively the exchange of persons, is limited primarily to those nations which are newly and rapidly rising into twentieth-century, industrialized society. These are the programs focused on national development, on economic and technological advance, and on the training of manpower for rapidly changing societies. They involve ordinarily long-range planning combined with immediate urgency, emphasizing a developmental approach in education as in other fields. They emphasize economic advancement, but with it also an urgent rise in literacy and the education of quality leadership.

This developmental area is one of the principal battlefields of the cold war, with Russia and the United States in direct competition in many sections of the world. The development and deployment of manpower under the Russian educational and social structure is claimed by the communists to be more effective for rapid, large-scale, industrial development than is our own system. We believe, on the contrary, that the democratic system, in education as in economics and politics, is advantageous. In this conflict, the adequate provision of education suitable as a means of accumulating trained manpower for national development is crucial. And there is considerable evidence that United States emphasis on education for individual development in the emerging states is considerably more effective and humanly appealing than the Russian educational approach.

ICA-AID programs

The inauguration of the Marshall Plan in 1948 and the announcement of a "Point Four Program" in President Truman's inaugural address in 1949, were followed by a series of executive orders and legislative acts culminating in the establishment of the International Cooperation Administration, more recently reorganized as the Agency for International Development. The agencies have been charged with the disbursement of foreign aid, and, of course, with the cooperative development of projects for which the aid is given. The development of highways and other transport facilities, of basic industries and power installations, of community development enterprises, of health and medical services, of education, have been concerns of the agencies. ICA and AID programs have been increasingly devoted to the processes of what Harlan Cleveland has called "institution building," and have been increasingly concerned with manpower training. The Congressional Act of 1961 which established AID stressed this in saying:

> In countries and areas which are in the earlier stages of economic development, programs of development of education and human resources through such means as technical cooperation shall be emphasized, and the furnishing of capital facilities for purposes other than the development of education and human resources shall be given a lower priority until the requisite knowledge and skills have been developed.

The foreign aid programs in education operate in a series of projects, undertaken always at the request of the host government, with the United States responsibilities sometimes discharged by regular AID staff and sometimes by contract with private agencies. Developmental loans or grants may be made, technical and supporting assistance given; projects may be developed through cooperation with a variety of international agencies. In all, AID directly employed in 1961 about 15,000 persons, of whom about 13,000 served overseas. Much of the responsibility for identifying projects, for evaluating plans, for administering operations, rests with this group of people. In Nigeria, for example, an AID Mission, attached to the United States Embassy, consisted in May, 1962, of 95 members. These included 20 administrative (including fiscal and personnel) officers and 75 program officers working directly on enterprises sponsored by AID. Some 20 of these program specialists were working on education projects.

The United States is obviously building up a corps of career specialists for overseas service in the fields of education, science, and culture. These specialists are to a considerable degree drawn from academic posts and share the interests of university faculties in both the scholarly and the professional fields. A corps of high calibre, dedicated to overseas service, is not easy to recruit and retain; there is considerable shift back and forth between government service and academic posts. Many of the best professional people in overseas government posts are there for limited periods on leave from their faculty positions. It seems advantageous for the government to appoint such persons wherever possible, and at the same time to facilitate in its career employees the research and publication activities which are ordinarily requisite to academic appointment and advancement. These emphases would make government careers more attractive to and feasible for many academically able persons. Moreover, research is fully as important in many of our overseas operations as it is within universities. The present small allocations for program research should be greatly extended for the ultimate benefit of the programs as well as to satisfy, for the personnel involved, the requirements for advancement in both government and university service.

University contracts

Beginning in 1951, the foreign aid agencies have developed a system of university contracts for overseas work which, on the whole, have been unusually successful. In these projects the ICA or AID representatives in a given country have negotiated agreements with the host government for an educational enterprise, and then have contracted with a United States university to carry on the work. In this way, schools of agriculture, or engineering, or public health, or public administration, or education have been organized; new universities in the land-grant pattern have been established, model secondary schools have been created; and a wide range of special educational services extending from adult extension projects to nursery schools, and from research facilitation to the expansion of audio-visual education services and to teaching English as a second language.

Again, Nigeria may be used as an illustration. In addition to the 95 officers under the direct employ of AID in Nigeria in 1962, nine contracts were in force, five of them with universities for educational work. Michigan State University, engaged in helping to establish a land-grant type university at Enugu, had a staff of 17 Americans on duty as faculty members and administrative officers. Ohio University had 11 persons on duty in connection with a secondary education program. University of California, Los Angeles, with contracts for helping to establish a government secondary school with a technical bias in Port Harcourt and a Federal Advanced Teachers College in Lagos, had seven staff members on assignment, with at least eight more to follow during the year. Indiana University had five persons working on audio-visual education and mass communication. Western Michigan University had a group of five specialists working on school services. In all, 46 persons were at work on educational enterprises, financed in part by AID funds, on contracts which made the 46 all employees of American universities.

The development of this contract system of operation presented many problems, both to the government agencies and to the universities. Only by trial-and-error, and through frustration and negotiation, were acceptable and sound contract principles developed. In general, the tendency has been toward an increased partnership by the university in the planning stages of a contract enterprise, and the covering of all university costs by the government. On the part of the university, regulations concerning placement, tenure, and retirement privileges have had to be modified so that faculty members can be assigned overseas without personal sacrifice. Detailed regulations covering procedures have been developed by the government, and universities have become increasingly conscious of their own responsibilities under the contract system. While there are inevitable irritations in the operations under any contract, the procedures work with increasing ease and efficiency.

The contractual arrangements by which universities undertake foreign service for AID, or for any other governmental agency, ought not to be entered into lightly by either side. Contract funds, contrary to the impression held by some faculties, are not grants-in-aid; the university under contract is not a completely free agent in the enterprise. No university should undertake a contract—and the government should be interested in no institution—unless the managerial arrangements, the specialist manpower, and the intent to serve are available. Any tendency in AID to distribute contracts among American universities on a geographical basis is to be condemned. The qualifications of a university for doing the job called for in the contract should be the only criterion, if the contract arrangement is to be efficient at home and successful abroad. The university should, if at all feasible, participate in the development of the project as the AID-foreign government contract is drafted, and should certainly make a preliminary survey prior to the drafting of the AID-university contract.

While any contract of this nature must be undertaken by the university as a public service in the national interest, originating in the new responsibilities of education, science, and culture in the relations among nations, the project undertaken should also have an academic value for the institution. Unless the project serves the faculty specialists in a geographic area or in the fields involved in the project, the university should not enter into the work. Projects which provide opportunity for research, for field study as well as field service, for internship experience of qualified younger men and women, are essential if the academic role of the university is to be safeguarded. Greater provision for these enterprises should be written into the contracts and the budgets than is now customary. At the same time, the university entering into a contract must be prepared to release faculty for overseas service without prejudice to normal employment rights, must respect fully the regulations of government on personnel and fiscal matters, and must be rigorous in evaluating the operation. The contractual relationship at its best is a partnership, with responsibility and respect on both sides.

THE PEACE CORPS

One of the newer federal agencies for overseas service—and one which operates extensively in the field of education—is the Peace Corps. Set up by Executive Order in 1961, financed at first from executive funds, it has won Congressional approval and seems likely to be a relatively permanent aspect of our foreign activity. On July 1, 1962, it had 973 Corpsmen assigned in 16 countries and 1,379 more in training in the United States. Operating during its first trial year on $30,000,000, Congress authorized expansion to a $63,750,000 budget level for its second year. Originally opposed and ridiculed by many critics, often on a partisan basis, it has won the present support of the major influences in the country.

The Peace Corps calls clearly to the same ethical and humane impulses in men and women on which the missionary movements of the centuries have been built. It is not simply an agency of sentiment; it calls for rigorous service in a variety of technical and professional fields. Since it is governmental in character, it operates within a political framework but has brought a new vivacity and enthusiasm to bureaucracy. It is under public scrutiny, and must be measured, in performance, against high standards. At first conceived as a Youth Corps, it calls heavily to the young, but has steadily widened its age range, and emphasized more its function as a service corps open to the qualified of all ages. In the group of 973 entering service in its first year, the average age was 24, but six persons were more than sixty years of age. It has become increasingly clear in the Peace Corps' operations that the service-minded generalist, young or old, is not needed as much as trained-for-service specialists of any age. The Corpsmen go to survey roads, to work in clinics and other public health services, to demonstrate effective methods of farming, to aid in community developments; they go as fishery experts and as teachers. Teaching accounts for the largest number; approximately two-thirds of the Corpsmen already assigned to projects are teachers.

The selection of Corpsmen is obviously crucial to the success of the Corps. Not only must individuals be well qualified for the specific work they are to do, but they must be psychologically mature. Misfits must be eliminated before they are sent abroad. On the whole, the record of the Corps in this respect is good. About four of every five admitted to training programs are sent overseas; of those sent over, only seven have been returned home, mostly for health reasons. The general image of the Corpsmen is that of able Americans, usually young men and women, not afraid to work, friendly, and knowledgeable about the work they are doing.

The selection of competent Corpsmen is sometimes difficult, particularly in the field of teaching. A common—and wrong—assumption among many of the early Corps officials was that anyone with a bachelor's degree could teach. In fact, it becomes increasingly clear that the most effective teachers abroad are the very ones who would be most effective in meeting professional requirements for teaching at home. The successful Corpsman must know well the subjects he is to teach, must be competent in managing a classroom and have psychological insight into the nature of learning, must know how to construct and use effective teaching aids, must have some knowledge of the country into which he is going, as well as of the nature and character of American education. He is in another country not only as a teacher, but inevitably also as a representative of the American educational tradition and practice.

It is in the interest of the Peace Corps to establish higher professional standards of selection for its prospective teachers. It should, wherever possible, secure teachers who are already experienced in the United States, or those who have secured professional as well as academic training for teaching. In this connection, the action of Boards of Education of, for example, New York and Los Angeles in guaranteeing tenure and retirement rights for their teachers who spend a tour of duty with the Peace Corps is highly important and commendable. The more of this the better. The experience of Corps service may be for many teachers extraordinarily rewarding; their value to the employing system and to the American children they teach is likely to be definitely higher after Peace Corps service. It should be possible, too, for the Peace Corps to cooperate with teacher-education institutions in programs where Corps service becomes almost an internship aspect of professional teacher education; the possibilities along this line have not yet been adequately explored.

The Peace Corps, in its rapid development, is encountering some of the difficulties of cooperating with colleges and universities which beset the predecessors of the Agency for International Development in their first enterprises. There is thus far a tendency in the Peace Corps simply to employ an educational institution to do a training job on an *ad hoc,* usually hurried basis, often under difficulties. The Corps finds it difficult as yet to accept universities as full partners in an educational enterprise; for this reason a number of universities, after an initial experience, have refused to accept second Peace Corps training contracts. Yet the guarantee of a continuing reservoir of particularly trained talent, in teaching and in the various technical fields, seems likely to lie, in the long run, in cooperative arrangements by which Peace Corps service is intimately related to professional training and status within the United States. It is highly desirable that the Peace Corps initiate experimental training projects along these lines in cooperation, so far as teachers are concerned, with American teacher-education institutions.

American and International Schools Abroad

A brief word should be said about American schools and international schools in which Americans are involved, located outside the United States. During the years since World War I, a good many such schools have been established to meet the needs of Americans and other expatriates living in cities overseas. In the early days of the League of Nations, an international school was established in Geneva to provide an elementary and secondary education for the children of League employees or diplomatic representatives stationed in Geneva who wanted to send their children back home for college. American schools have been established in Paris and Rome to serve the needs of the American colonies there and the children of other nationalities seeking an American education. Throughout Latin America, schools for the children of United States parents resident there have been established—some as schools for the employees of an industry, some as missionary schools, some as independent schools created by a group of parents. Many American firms find it necessary to maintain schools at their installations abroad in order to attract the personnel they want. The same is true for American personnel in foreign service, including the military service, in the AID programs, and at the headquarters of international organizations.

A directory of International and American schools around the world, prepared by the International Schools Foundation indicates that there are 53 such schools in Latin America, 38 in Asia, and 24 in Europe. One exists in connection with the secretariat of the United Nations in New York City. The schools serve an important function for the government, for industries, for international organizations—for any agency which has the task of recruiting personnel for service outside the homeland. And, in addition to these, there are the schools set up by military occupation authorities after World War II to serve their personnel abroad.

American schools abroad ordinarily labor under financial burdens and difficulties in recruiting faculty. The International Schools Foundation was created by a group of citizens in 1955 to aid in channeling philanthropic gifts to such schools, and to provide a professional service in faculty recruitment, curriculum improvement, and consultation. For some years the federal government, through a grant to the American Council on Education, has supported an association of the American schools in Latin America with professional services. More recently it has given grants-in-aid for the construction of buildings to a number of the American schools in cities where there is a large American population. Support of these institutions is desirable, both because they meet the needs of American communities abroad and because, in some situations, they become model and experimental institutions, influential in the educational development of their areas.

It is desirable that schools of this type be made available on a larger scale than at present in the developing countries where AID and other diplomatic and technical agencies need many American families. Such schools should, however, not be restricted to American students. They could well be developed as model institutions in the American pattern, serving a double purpose, linked to the educational enterprises for the development of a new area and to the educational needs of the United States personnel. In various cities of Asia and Africa, for example, such schools could be highly advantageous as meeting grounds for parents of the host and the visiting nationalities, forums for the discussion of educational concepts, and influences in the development of the country concerned.

INTERNATIONAL ORGANIZATIONS

UNESCO

At the close of World War II, the United States exercised considerable leadership in establishing UNESCO as one of the specialized agencies of the United Nations. The new organization was intended to advance the fields of education, science, and culture through international enterprises, to promote enlightenment in the shadowed areas of the earth, and to apply the fruits of learning to human betterment. The organization got off to a sentimental start in the United States, and was in some respects overestimated as an agency to prevent the recurrence of war. It became an object of controversy for the American public, but support of its programs has been consistent and non-partisan so far as governmental policy has been concerned. In the 16 years of its existence, UNESCO's budget has grown substantially; its program has weathered much trial and error, and it has established itself as one of the international agencies capable of long-range contribution to human welfare. In general, American participation in its work has been both high-minded and, particularly since the U.S.S.R. has joined UNESCO, politically effective.

In spite of the efforts of many individuals, the United States National Commission for UNESCO which was created as a democratic political invention linking the "educational, scientific, and cultural forces" of the country with the government has not functioned as a coordinating force for activities in cultural relations with other countries to the degree originally anticipated. In recent years, however, the Commission's schedule for participation in advising on the development of the UNESCO program has been improved. In particular, its biennial national conferences have become more effective as they have focused on topics of major consequence. The Commission itself is a useful channel of communication between government and non-governmental organizations, capable of greater stimulation and influence than it has thus far shown.

Through much of UNESCO's history, the United States, both officially and in public opinion, has viewed the organization to a considerable extent only as an agency for helping good causes in other parts of the world. We were generous, for example, in the UNESCO programs for educational rehabilitation in war-damaged areas during the early postwar years. We took the initiative in 1960 in stimulating the organization into a large program of educational development in Africa. We refrained consistently until very recent years in seeking UNESCO fellowships for Americans, and in general asked little of the organization for ourselves. The UNESCO enterprises we supported were generally advantageous, and our support of them was important, but, in the long run, every member state, including the United States, should ask how it profits from the existence and the program of the organization. The United States has been aided by UNESCO in many ways—and these aids should be of primary importance in American evaluation of the program. The United States is now nominating Americans for UNESCO fellowships. The organization's program of publications is examined in terms of what it contributes to the scholarly interests of this country. A more realistic appraisal of the values of our continued membership in the organization is now under way.

UNESCO serves as the operating agency for many of the educational projects financed by the United Nations Special Fund. Many of these projects in underdeveloped areas may be advantaged by close cooperation between UNESCO and such national agencies as AID. In Nigeria, for example, the Federal Advanced Teachers College now under development in Lagos, involves the acquisition of land by the Nigerian government, the construction of buildings with grants from the United Nation's Special Fund through UNESCO and AID, the provision of library development by private foundations, and the provision of faculty by UNESCO (again operating for the Special Fund), and the University of California, Los Angeles (acting under contract with AID). These cooperative arrangements are exceedingly complex, and their success is ultimately dependent on full cooperation among field personnel. But there needs to be exhaustive study of the contractual and administrative provisions by which these bilateral and multilateral operations can be more effectively intermeshed.

A major portion of UNESCO's work is in the field of education, as indicated both by its budget and by analysis of its enterprises. A good many American educators have participated in these program operations. In the field of comparative education, for example, American scholars are greatly aided by the efforts UNESCO has made to secure the reporting of educational statistics on an international and comparative basis. In recent years UNESCO has emphasized regional educational planning as its particular task. A series of conferences of the Ministers of Education of American States have focused attention on the continental problems of education and have outlined a framework in which national educational developments can be mutually supporting. Similar planning conferences have been held in Asia and in South America. While regional planning is certainly useful, and UNESCO is distinctively qualified to take the initiative in it, the planning should not be mistaken for actual achievement—and achievement occurs primarily within national rather than regional bounds.

International bureau of education

Well before World War II and the establishment of UNESCO in 1946, an International Bureau of Education had been established in Geneva. With an ill-defined membership of various governments, but with financial aid from Switzerland and under the leadership of Jean Piaget, the Bureau assembled a pedagogical library, issued a series of publications, and held annual conferences on educational topics. Its yearbooks provided a useful summary of recent educational developments in the nations represented at its conferences.

As UNESCO came into being, a relationship between it and the Bureau was worked out. The Bureau continued as an autonomous unit, regularized its own governmental membership and dues, interchanged its personnel with UNESCO, and was largely financed through UNESCO. The United States became a regular member of the Bureau in 1958. The annual conferences held by the Bureau under UNESCO sponsorship have become increasingly important to international educational relations, as have the Bureau's publications, which are among the best resources for the comparative study of education. United States participation in the Bureau's work has been effective and advantageous.

International regional organizations

The Organization of American States (OAS) has long maintained an educational and cultural program within its secretariat, the Pan-American Union. It has published materials useful to schools and to scholars, has facilitated the translation and dissemination of educational documents among member states, and has from time to time established special commissions or committees to work on particular fields and problems.

Generally speaking, however, the OAS action programs in education have not reached the level of effectiveness of either UNESCO or the Agency for International Development. While the major part of United States educational relations with Latin American countries through the Alliance for Progress will likely continue on a bilateral basis or through UNESCO's multilateral enterprises, it would also seem highly advantageous to strengthen the educational efforts of the Organization of American States. A series of field enterprises in education conducted cooperatively, as distinguished from office or conference undertakings, would be appropriate and advantageous for the Organization.

The North Atlantic Treaty Organization (NATO) and the South East Asia Treaty Organization (SEATO), though military alliances, have undertaken extensive educational work. Recognizing the importance of mutual understanding in the maintenance of an alliance, NATO and SEATO have organized cultural conferences among their members, have established exchange fellowships and have supported scholarly research on cultural matters related to the alliances. Their educational programs, however, operated largely through voluntary councils in member states and without large financing, have been developed with difficulty. The military basis of the organizations makes cultural program development extremely difficult, but at the same time the very efforts toward such programs symbolizes the new relationship between education and international action.

Cultural conventions

During the years between the two World Wars, a number of European nations developed bi-national cultural agreements or conventions. These agreements, formal in character, ordinarily stressed mutual cultural interests, arranged for cultural exchanges, including exchange of persons, and regularized joint efforts in cultural matters. Both France and Great Britain took active interest in these conventions, and out of them came a network of consciously-stimulated cultural ties, particularly among European states. Such conventions reached a high level of development in the framework of the Northern Association of Scandinavian Countries.

The United States did not at first enter into conventions of this character, primarily because the role of the federal government in cultural and educational matters was not clear. At the Seventh International Conference of American States, held in Montevideo in 1933, and again at the 1936 Inter-American Conference for the Maintenance of Peace, held in Buenos Aires, a convention was adopted calling for the improvement of school programs to the end of developing mutual understanding among American States. The United States at first opposed the convention, but later ratified it. Under its terms the federal government granted funds to the American Council on Education in 1938 to conduct the study, *Latin America in School and College Teaching Materials*.

After a protracted period of difficulties in U.S.A.-U.S.S.R. relations, the governments of the two countries authorized negotiations which began in late 1957 and resulted in January 1958 in an Exchange Agreement. Designed to open up cultural channels between the two countries, the Agreement authorized exchanges in "the cultural, technical and educational fields." Basic arrangements for exchanges of radio and television broadcasts, of "specialists in Industry, Agriculture and Medicine," of "cultural, civic, youth and student groups," of parliamentary delegations, of scientists, of "theatrical, choral and choreographic groups, symphony orchestras and artistic performers," of athletes and sports teams, of "university delegations," of exhibits and publications, were outlined in the convention. While many problems plagued the development of some of the exchanges, the program on the whole was an asset to both countries. The Agreement was renewed and, in some ways, expanded in 1962.

It seems desirable that the United States should extend its bilateral cultural relations programs by further development of specific cultural agreements. An agreement between Canada and the United States is in many ways desirable. During World War II the Carnegie Endowment for International Peace took the initiative in organizing a non-governmental Canadian-American Committee on Education, with members representing educational groups in the two countries. The Committee, with joint Chairmen and Secretaries, made surveys of the treatment of each country in the school textbooks of the other, prepared the only comprehensive catalogue of educational exchanges between the two countries, examined some of the perplexing questions of interchange of books, magazines, teaching materials, films, and radio programs, and prepared statements about the relations of the two countries appropriate for school curricula. The Committee did an excellent job with the meager resources it had available, but it has now passed out of existence. While the relations of the two countries are excellent, there continue to be certain frustrations of interchange and lack of complete understanding. In order to maintain the best of relations between the two countries, a basic core of cultural relations should be guaranteed by the governments, and a channel of continuing communication through a responsible bi-national committee on educational and cultural relations should be established. Such a committee could function effectively as a preventive of misunderstanding.

Even more complex is the problem of our educational relations with Mexico. The relations between the organized education groups of the two countries are currently at low ebb. It would be advantageous to explore fully the possibility of sustaining educational and cultural relations between the two neighbors by an active program specifically outlined in a formal agreement.

THE NEED FOR RESEARCH

From all the developments and enterprises to which reference has been made in this chapter, one general conclusion must be drawn—there is urgent need for evaluation and assessment. In a sense, most nations have operated and are operating in the international educational field on the basis of unverified assumptions; most of our procedures are *ad hoc,* created to meet a situation, devised on the basis of hunch and intuition which may or may not be valid. Too little is known about the actual relation of education to economic development; too little is known about the processes and conditions under which educational ideas and institutions are transplanted successfully across cultural lines. There should be included in all of our international educational programs a large measure of research focused on the analysis of the programs themselves. The experiences of all nations in this field during this century have gone too long unanalyzed. We continue to play our cultural relations programs by ear, because the music has not been structured and written down in terms of rigidly evaluated experience.

There is a slowly growing research literature bearing on the exchange of persons. But the excellent beginning in this analysis which was made by the Social Science Research Council a decade ago has not adequately been followed up. The relation of personality to a successful experience as a foreign student, the phases through which one goes during a year's sojourn abroad, the causes of tension or of security among foreign students, the prognosis of success among foreign students—these are matters on which we have too little information to enable us to determine policies and guide practices.

In the techniques of international educational action we have hardly begun a research program. If, for example, we are faced with the problem of planning our educational relations with Turkey, we will find little analysis recorded of our long educational relations with that country. What has been the influence of Robert College as an American transplantation in Istanbul? Why did the book-length report by John Dewey, imported by Attaturk to prepare a plan for the development of Turkish education, have no visible influence on subsequent developments? Is it sensible to try to create a land-grant university, with American aid, in the mountain areas of Erzerum? Or would it be a wiser investment of American aid to enlarge the literacy program for army conscripts, or to develop a model comprehensive high school? What have been the results of the Ford Foundation's substantial investment in a Turkish National Commission on Education, designed to outline educational priorities for the 1960's? Lack of searching answers to such questions is a difficult handicap in planning AID operations in Turkey, or for determining Turkish needs from American aid, or of determining long-range policy for Turkish educational development. A series of national case studies of American educational activities and enterprises abroad might begin to give us the data on which to predict relative degrees of success and failure in future programs. There is every reason to hope that AID funds and the Cooperative Research funds of the United States Office of Education, as well as foundation grants, will be earmarked for the urgent development of a basic literature in this field.

The rise of comparative studies in education, now under way in various university centers and governmental agencies around the world, is a promising development in this area of needed research. In the University of London, in Moscow, in Kyushu, in the Hamburg Institute of Education, in the Japanese Ministry of Education and the United States Office of Education, and in some six or eight American universities, programs of research or advanced-level instruction in comparative education have been developed since World War II. Drawing heavily on the behavioral sciences and on history, these centers are all engaged in studies of educational problems common among nations, of the relation of education to economic development, of the procedures of international educational exchange. UNESCO has become a gatherer of educational data from all nations, and has moved steadily toward an accumulation of quantitative information about education on a basis making international analyses and comparisons possible. UNESCO now plans to convene in 1963 the first international conference on comparative education. In the further development of comparative education we may gain research data of consequence in the planning of national programs and at the same time produce a more adequate supply of qualified persons for work in this field.

TECHNOLOGICAL DEVELOPMENTS IN EDUCATION

In telescoping centuries of national growth into decades, the applications of technology to education may be of much greater effectiveness in the emerging nations than has thus far been recognized. In various sections of Africa, for example, it may be more feasible to attack illiteracy by putting television screens in remote villages and beaming educational programs to them than to establish immediately "a school in every village" and to provide the teaching staff for such schools. It may be easier to provide a film on the government of Nigeria for use in all that country's schools than to train all the teachers to give the instruction on government. In some areas and for many subjects it may be more efficient to develop a library of films—or perhaps of microfilms—than a library of books. The recent exploits of Telstar indicate something of the possibilities as well as the problems in international education by television.

In virtually all of the developing countries, the provision of teaching materials in adequate supply is an enormously difficult task. In meeting the need one is faced with the desirability of using resources immediately available, such as paper, maps, books, pictures, etc., and on the other hand adapting the newer machines such as films and television which, at their best, may utilize the fruits of "programmed instruction." Programmed instruction is not merely instruction recorded on tape or film, but a more carefully developed sequence of learnings, with scrupulous attention to the relationship between the goals of instruction and the precise subject matter presented. The newer "teaching machines" make more possible than ever before an experimentally verified curriculum— and it is this curriculum which may be built into the educational planning of many of the emerging states.

What is needed, then, is a creative approach to the provision of the most effective teaching materials in the schools and colleges that the United States is aiding in the emerging countries. This creativity needs to extend from the production of teaching materials—even laboratory materials—out of the resources available in the local environment to the importation of the latest innovations of a mass-communication, electronically, technologically dominated age. UNESCO has convened one session of specialists to examine these possibilities in their international setting. AID and the Office of Education have begun exploration of the problems and possibilities in this field. The United States National Commission for UNESCO has recently convened a short seminar of experts to advise on the use of technical aids in African education. It is highly desirable for universities operating abroad under AID contracts to develop imaginative proposals in this area. To do so requires an unusual combination of practical sagacity and technological competence, but in this area major break-throughs may be anticipated—and welcomed—during the coming decade.

AMERICAN NEEDS AND INTERNATIONAL RESOURCES

As has been indicated, much of American educational activity abroad has been undertaken for high humanitarian motives or for considerations of developing democratic allies, but not always with enough attention to the current educational needs and interests of the United States itself. Both the altruism and the political motivation are often misinterpreted abroad. It may well be that the position of the United States will be strengthened by a well formulated, long-range policy of self-interest in educational matters. We have talked much of the desirability of a "two-way street" in our international cultural and educational relations. To implement this two-way concept by emphasizing more than we have the flow of useful materials from abroad to the United States may be a wise policy.

It has been suggested earlier in this chapter that the universities of the United States should give institutional needs and developments a greater role in their endorsement of Fulbright applications than they now do, and that the national committees making final Fulbright awards should consider fully the intellectual and cultural interests of the United States. It has also been suggested that the United States should endorse more fully the UNESCO operations which are particularly beneficial to American education. It has been suggested, too, that American universities which accept AID contracts should do so only when the university has the resources for fulfilling the contracts and is also advantaged in some academic fashion by the contracts. These suggestions have been made not in the interest of a narrow American self-interest, but as a realistic implementation of the ultimate necessity of a two-way flow in international cultural and educational affairs. It is not sufficient either for the donor or the receiver of educational aid abroad to have the process primarily a one-way contribution.

In many areas of the world, both primitive and advanced, the role of folk music and folk dance is far more effective in educational programs than are music and the dance in American education. What can we learn from these societies? American educational authorities are now stressing facility in a second language for an increasing number of Americans. What can we learn from the educational experience of other countries in which a second language for university people has long been accepted as a necessity? What has been the experience in other countries on the relationship between church and state in educational matters? Have any Fulbright awards been made with the intent of enlightening us on this basic question in American education?

Self-interest, if it be at the scholarly and professional level, is a legitimate value. We ourselves may be enriched by international cultural activities which recognize this fact, and, at the same time, we shall be better accepted abroad and may more effectively emphasize the two-way aspect of exchange.

AN EXPERIMENTAL APPROACH

It is possible that new developments and potentialities inherent in education's role in international affairs cannot be satisfied adequately by dependence upon traditional institutions. The needs for creativity in the use of communication devices and programmed learning may be paralleled by a need for creativity in the development of new educational institutions. The U.S.S.R. is experimenting with a special university—Friendship University—for foreign students in Moscow, and proposals are occasionally put forward for development of such an institution in the United States. While full information concerning Friendship University is not available, what is known is not, on the whole, favorable. Foreign students want to mix with native students and attend the same institutions they attend; to separate the foreign students from the ordinary currents of academic work provokes resentment. The university for foreigners is almost inevitably tarred with the brush of "second-rate" education. Friendship University does provide for a period of intensive language instruction. This is particularly important to the degree that the language of a country is not learned by students before their foreign sojourn. While facility in English continues to be a problem for foreign students in the United States, a very large proportion of the students have studied English before their arrival. Brief training periods are desirable, but the prevalence of English as a second tongue around the world makes it feasible for the United States to insist increasingly on language facility prior to arrival in this country. In many of the manpower-development programs sponsored by AID and other agencies, the teaching of English as a second language is emphasized. Because of these conditions no American counterpart of Friendship University seems desirable.

Within the United States, two developments have taken place in recent years in the adjustment of educational institutions to international needs. The East-West Center attached to the University of Hawaii and supported by federal funds is designed as a meeting ground for students and scholars from Asia and from continental America. The early organizational difficulties of the Center have now been overcome, and a program outlined which seems attractive to many students. Built into the program, fortunately, are opportunities by which Asians at the Center make field trips onto the American continent and Americans at the Center have opportunities for field work in Asia. On a smaller scale, the University of Puerto Rico has developed programs emphasizing its potential as a meeting ground for representatives of the cultures of North and South America.

It is possible, as suggested earlier in this chapter, that the established junior colleges of the United States, particularly in their terminal vocational programs, may play a more important role as host to foreign students than heretofore. Certainly the possibilities in this field should be creatively explored. And the extent to which the concepts of the American junior colleges can be utilized in newly industrialized areas is a matter to which AID should give further attention.

While it is possible that new institutions may be conceived to perform better the tasks of contemporary education, it is most likely that the greatest success in the immediate future will be found in the modification of existing institutions. American universities, internally, can do much to improve their own adjustments under the impact of world affairs. In recent years some universities have attempted to coordinate and strengthen their programs by the establishment of over-all policy committees and offices of deans or directors of the institution's own international affairs. Indeed, a significant body of literature is beginning to emerge dealing with the impact of world affairs on institutions of higher education. In these studies and in the efforts to make existing institutional activities more efficient lies much hope for the immediate future.

CONCLUSION

It is obvious, as one surveys developments of the twentieth century either as educator or as diplomat, that modern states are beginning a new chapter in their dealings with each other within the framework of education, foreign policy, and international affairs. In this chapter, the role of education will be increasingly significant and much more complex than is often assumed. Programs of international educational action are, to a considerable extent, still in an exploratory stage, in a "freshman period." The need for penetrating and continuing research and appraisal of experience in this area is steadily mounting. While the programs carried on either multilaterally or bilaterally have been and are deeply influenced by the pressures of the cold war, the movement for planned educational relations among states is far more than an incident in the competitions among nations. There is a deeper trend in human affairs toward the application of education to developmental needs, toward the satisfaction of wide-stirring aspirations, toward the advancement of learning on a scale commensurate with the problems of world prosperity and peace. This deeper trend should be the essential focus for educational planning in international matters. Education is inherently a long-range investment, and education's role in foreign affairs is best determined in terms of long-range policy.

Roger Revelle

4

International Cooperation and the Two Faces of Science

Many shall run to and fro,
and knowledge shall be increased.
                    (Daniel 12.4)

THE TWO ASPECTS OF SCIENCE

Science has two aspects: one is the search for truth—the attempt to gain understanding of the world about us and of ourselves; the other is the use of knowledge to gain control over nature and power over men.

The search for truth

In its aspect of the search for truth, international cooperation in science is a contradiction in terms. The search for truth is not national, it is personal and individual; hence it cannot be international in the sense of relations between nations. The work of individual scientists finds its meaning in the context of the work of their predecessors, their contemporaries, and their successors throughout the community of science. This

ROGER REVELLE, *director of the Scripps Institution of Oceanography, University of California, is currently on leave from that post to serve as science adviser to the Secretary of the Interior. Dr. Revelle has been head of the Geophysics Branch, Office of Naval Research; member of the United States Commission for UNESCO and of panels of the President's Science Advisory Committee. He has also been United States delegate to many international conferences.*

community cuts across national boundaries, and, indeed, is as wide as the great globe itself, just as its objects of study are as wide as the universe.

Nor is scientific excellence the exclusive possession of any one nation or group of nations; the talents and capabilities of scientists in many lands constitute a valuable resource for all nations. Cooperation among scientists of different countries in the search for truth is, therefore, as old as science. The language, methods, and ethics of this search are universal; its only limitations are those of the human mind. Because of the unity and interdependence of science, it transcends differences in political and social systems and is supra-national.

The supra-national values that guide scientists in their search for truth conflict at times with the foreign policies of nations; resolution of such conflicts calls for statesmanship of a high order. Cooperation in scientific truth-seeking can be a powerful tool for building understanding among the peoples of the world only if its cohesive international force is aided by national attitudes, policies, and actions.

A structure of world-wide relationships is essential for progress in the search for truth. Major areas of inquiry, such as geophysics, meteorology, oceanography, animal and human ecology, astrophysics, and public health take most meaningful form only on a global framework. Hurricanes, droughts, and pestilence know no national boundaries.

The world contains phenomena far beyond what is available within any single country, and distant parts of the earth must be the stage for much scientific research. In botany, for example, a transect around the world along the 45th parallel would constitute virtually a controlled experiment. In this latitude lie such diverse environments as the vineyards of Bordeaux, the smiling valley of the Po, the mouths of the Danube, the Crimean beach resorts of the Soviet Union, Mongolia's Gobi Desert, and the northern tip of Japan's frigid island of Hokkaido. In the United States, the 45th parallel stretches from the mild and rainy coast of Oregon across the plains of Dakota to the tip of Maine. These various environments have one thing in common—the number of hours of daylight and darkness at different seasons throughout the year. Yet there is a pine tree, called the Mugo Pine, that reproduces naturally in many places, but only near this latitude. Evidently the tree's specific character is determined by photoperiodism, and not by temperature or humidity, or other climatic factors.

The control over nature

Science has another purpose besides the striving for truth: this is control over the forces of nature, hopefully for the welfare of mankind. It is a truism to say that in our times the applications of science and technology are exerting a revolutionary influence on men and nations. Science and technology today give power, not only over the external world, but also over other human beings. This is the chief reason why the leaders of modern governments are concerned with science. The sovereigns of the Middle Ages employed alchemists in a desperate attempt to replenish their empty treasuries; the governments of today support research largely because a continually advancing technology is essential for military security and economic growth.

In this aspect of their work, scientists are primarily citizens. Their discoveries determine the policies of governments, and governments, in turn, profoundly influence the course of science.

In the enlightened 18th century, a learned man could separate his scientific work from his political life. Benjamin Franklin must have been thinking as a Fellow of the Royal Society, even though he was Postmaster General of the revolting Colonies, when he issued an order that American ships should give aid and comfort to Captain James Cook. Lavoisier's head was cut off because he was on the wrong side politically, even while the world honored him for his chemical discoveries.

Few scientists in our era of scientific revolution can search for truth from an ivory tower. In their work, as in their lives, they must first be citizens of a country. To a greater degree than ever before, they are in the position of Socrates when he heard humming in his ears, like the sound of the flute in the ears of the mystic, the voices of the law that kept him from hearing any other as they said, "He who disobeys us is, as we maintain, thrice wrong. . . ."

Science and politics

Even if they wanted to, today's scientists could not be indifferent to public affairs; their welfare and their opportunities for accomplishment are too closely interwoven with the lives of nations and the world of politics. As a consequence, many scientists are having to assume a quasi-political role.

This is not to say that modern politics and modern science are the same thing; on the contrary, they rest on quite different foundations. Science proceeds step-wise from the known to the unknown, transferring at each step from the particular to the general and back again, building at each step a model of understanding that can be used to generalize, to unify, and to predict. The successful scientist attacks only those problems he feels able to solve, problems on the frontier of knowledge but ready for solution. The politician deals always with the unknown future. He cannot select problems that are solvable; his problems are thrust upon him by the force of events. He must base his actions not on rational understanding but on experience and insight. He deals with intangibles, with the mysteries of human motives and emotions; he can see only a short distance into the future, and, even so, through a glass darkly.

The essence of politics is that it deals with particular problems, not with generalities, and with unique problems that are never exactly the same as those that have arisen before. The results of political action are always uncertain; the effective politician must always be prepared to alter his actions in the light of events. He knows better than most scientists that men do not behave reasonably, but in accordance with the patterns of their culture, that the human mind is not the logical machine described by Aristotle, but follows quite different and, as yet unknown laws.

From the political standpoint of today, international cooperation in science and technology should have many virtues. In former times, mutual understanding between scientists of different countries had little relevance for the mass of their compatriots. Now scientists in their quasi-political roles can contribute effectively toward elimination of suspicion and prejudice. More important, international cooperation provides the free exchange of ideas that is essential for rapid technical progress. Politicians and diplomats have gradually come to a partial understanding of these facts. But in their nation-structured world the scientist, like the artist, is bound to be suspect because of the supra-national nature of his interests. How can a man who believes that truth is universal, while he is at the same time skeptical about his own possession of it, be trusted to be single-mindedly loyal to one nation? Moreover, statesmen look with marked distaste on the fact that their most cherished and time-tested policies can be nullified by scientific discoveries which they can neither control nor predict.

Today, as in the recent past, the secrecy imposed by national security considerations impedes much potential international cooperation in science, even though it can be argued from the history of atomic weapons that secrecy does not guarantee security. The suspicions engendered by secrecy may in fact lead to a dangerous instability in the precarious equilibrium of terror under which we live. An open world may be the only world that can survive in a technological age.

Expanding science and shrinking world

Science itself, both as truth-seeker and as controller of nature, has contributed to the widespread recognition of the need for cooperation among nations. Jet aircraft and high-speed communication have shrunk the human world. The astronauts and the International Geophysical Year have helped men everywhere to feel in their bellies, not just on the edges of their minds, that the earth is a planet, isolated and complete in itself, and that we who travel on it must work together if we are to survive.

The accelerating changes brought about by technology are obvious to everyone. But the growth of the scientific enterprise that has produced these changes is little known. On the average in advanced countries, the numbers of scientists and technicians have been doubling every decade.

At the beginning of the 19th century, the total number of scientific and technical journals was roughly 100; by 1850 it reached about 1,000; by 1900 it was 10,000. Now it is 100,000. If the rate of growth continues, we may expect a million scientific periodicals by the end of this century. This exponential proliferation of scientific information menaces the unity, and hence the very existence of science as we have known it. Science is in danger of a kind of suicide either by self-suffocation or by tearing itself into isolated fragments.

Of course, other forms of human activity are also increasing, but at a slower rate. The doubling time of activities not directly related to science is 20 to 40 years. Such a difference can hardly be maintained throughout the next century.

Kinds of International Scientific Cooperation

Like every aspect of science, international scientific cooperation has burgeoned mightily during the last fifteen years, and we have learned a good deal about its blessings and defects.

The most important and valuable kind of cooperation is simply to facilitate communication between scientists of different countries. This can take many forms: organization and support of international congresses, conferences, and symposia; establishment of international scientific journals, abstracting and translation services; direct exchange of persons, from graduate students to senior scientists; facilitation of such exchanges by compiling directories and publicizing opportunities, as well as by financial support; exchanges of data which can be used to test hypotheses and theories; exchanges of instruments and techniques; development of the specialized languages of science by international agreements on nomenclature and the definition of terms.

International scientific meetings

Since World War II, all these aids to communication have greatly increased. For example, it is estimated that each year between 15,000 and 20,000 United States scientists and engineers attend 2,000 international meetings where they have personal contact with some hundred thousand of their colleagues from other countries.

Face-to-face meetings among scientists, whether in each other's laboratories, in informal symposia, or in international congresses, are a most effective means for exchange of scientific information and ideas. One of the reasons such meetings are essential is the overwhelming tide of scientific publications described above, which forces even the most rapid reader to concentrate on a microscopically narrow range of interest. But there are at least three other reasons.

The first, not generally recognized by laymen, is the fact that good art and good science have much in common. Both depend on a seeing eye and on imagination. The artist and the scientist must be able to see things that other people do not see, and to find relationships, through the free association we call imagination, between things that have never been related before. As with many arts, a good deal of science can not be communicated, much less taught, except through direct personal contact. This is particularly true of experimental techniques. Details of experimental procedure are hard to describe in words and are rarely published; they must be seen to be believed.

The second reason is also contrary to common belief: scientific ideas are usually born in conversation, rather than in the mind of one man. The rigorous thinking needed to nurse a new-born idea into a useful hypothesis must almost always be done in private. But the fresh insights, the new associations between previously unrelated phenomena, often come from the interplay of two or three minds clashing in conversation.

Even more important is the fact that, in talking face to face, scientists allow themselves to state their intuitions and partly-formulated ideas, unconstrained by the caution they demand in the printed word. Custom requires that the usual scientific meeting shall center around a series of formal papers. But just as graduate students often learn more from each other than from their professors, so mature scientists learn from informal discussion in the lobby as much as from the lecture in the auditorium.

Exchange of students and research workers

Exchange of scientists at its best implies free movement across national boundaries for study, teaching, research, and the sharing of knowledge.

Only the first steps toward free exchange have been taken in the relations between the United States and the Soviet Union. The National Academy of Sciences of the United States and the Academy of Sciences of the U.S.S.R. have entered into an agreement under which a few dozen scientists of various levels of distinction and experience have been exchanged on a *quid pro quo* basis. In comparison with the total numbers of foreign students and faculty members in the United States and the corresponding numbers of Americans abroad, the extent of exchanges with the Soviet Union is infinitesimal. According to *Open Doors 1962,* published by the Institute of International Education, out of the 58,086 foreign students in the United States in 1961-62, 37 were from the U.S.S.R.; 37 out of 19,836 American overseas students attended Soviet educational institutions. Of the 5,530 faculty members from other countries who spent a major part of the year in the United States 9 were Soviet citizens. Of the 2,427 American university faculty members who taught and did research abroad only 22 made an extended visit to the U.S.S.R. Seven of these were social scientists, 1 was a specialist in humanities, 8 were in medicine, and 5 were natural scientists.

On a world-wide and over-all basis the numbers of foreign students and faculty members in the United States, and the numbers of Americans overseas are quite impressive. In 1961-62, over 72,000 foreign citizens studied or did research at American universities, colleges, and hospitals. This was an 80 percent increase over 1955. The number of foreign faculty members and advance researchers on United States campuses was eight times the number in 1955. Of the foreign citizens in the United States, 8,500, or 12 percent, were medical interns and residents affiliated with United States hospitals, while 80 percent were students at 1800 American universities and colleges. About half of these were enrolled as undergraduates and 42 percent as graduates.

The number of American scholars overseas was a third of the number of foreign citizens in American campuses and hospitals. Five hundred and ninety institutions in 66 foreign countries were hosts to United States students, and American faculty members from over 400 universities and colleges taught or carried out research in 90 countries. The number of United States faculty members abroad increased by a third between 1957-58 and 1961-62.

Analysis of these figures shows some marked imbalances. Also United States institutions in 50 states, the District of Columbia, Puerto Rico, and Guam reported foreign students on their campuses, more than a third of these students was in only 23 universities. One out of six students in Howard University was from overseas, one out of eight at MIT, and one out of 13 at Harvard, while in some southern universities, only one out of 200 students came from outside the United States.

Only between the United States and Western Europe is there a genuine two-way flow of scholars and students. During 1961-62, more than 9,000 Europeans studied or taught in the United States, and 11,000 Americans worked in the Western European countries. In contrast, 80 percent of the foreign students and scholars in the United States came from the Far East, Latin America, the Near and Middle East, and Africa, while only about 20 percent of the Americans went to these areas. In 1960-61, there were 100 times as many Chinese in the United States as Americans in Taiwan and Hong Kong, 40 times as many Indians in the United States as Americans in India, and 10 times as many Japanese here as Americans in Japan. On the other hand, there were five times more Americans in France than Frenchmen in the United States, four times as many Americans in Switzerland and Austria, and twice as many in Germany as the numbers of citizens of those countries in the United States.

During 1961-62 more than 50 per cent of the foreign students on United States campuses majored in engineering, natural and physical sciences, medicine, or agriculture, and about 19 per cent in the humanities and 14 per cent in the social sciences. Over half of the American students abroad were concerned with the humanities, including creative and liberal arts, languages and literature, and theology, and only about a fourth with sciences, medicine, engineering and agriculture. The attraction of the United States for persons interested in the sciences and related fields is also seen in the figures for foreign faculty members in this country, of whom 74 per cent were in the natural and physical sciences, medicine, engineering, and agriculture. Only 38 per cent of the American scholars overseas were in these fields.

It may be of interest to academic administrators to note that the student-faculty ratio of foreign citizens in the United States is about 11 to 1, whereas the ratio of American students to American faculty members abroad is only about 8 to 1. If these ratios were to remain constant while the total number of exchanges continued its exponential rise, American faculty members left at home might eventually start to complain about their added teaching loads.

The distribution of students by fields of study on a world-wide basis, as revealed by *Study Abroad* published by UNESCO in 1961, is very similar to that of foreign students in the United States. About 12 per cent in 1960-61 were in the natural sciences, 16 per cent in medicine, 22 per cent in engineering, and 3 per cent in agriculture, giving a total of 52.7 per cent in scientific and technical fields, compared with 17 per cent who were studying law or social sciences, and 24 per cent in humanities and education.

The U.S.S.R. does not publish any data on the countries of origin of its foreign students or on their fields of study. However, such data are available from Bulgaria, Hungary, Poland, and Czechoslovakia. In all four countries, 75 per cent to more than 80 per cent of the students were in the natural sciences, engineering, medicine, or agriculture, and 80 per cent to 90 per cent of the students were in these fields plus the social sciences. As in the United States, other countries report very small numbers of students from the Soviet Union, the total in 18 of the principal countries receiving foreign students being only about 300. There were 39 Soviet students in the Vatican, two and a half times the number in the United States for the same year.

More than half of the foreign students in the world's universities and colleges are at least partly supported by fellowships and travel grants. 115,000 such awards were reported to UNESCO in 1960-61, nearly six times the number in 1948-49. At present the number of fellowships is apparently doubling every eight years. One sixth of these are offered by the United Nations and other international organizations, about half by governments, and the remainder by foundations, educational institutions, and other private organizations. As might be expected, the largest proportion of fellowship programs, 31 per cent, is in basic and applied sciences, but about 25 per cent of all programs, representing a total of some 50,000 individual awards, are not restricted to any particular field.

Over 300 universities and colleges in the United States and nearly 200 foundations, ranging from the Texas-Swedish Cultural Foundation to the Institute of World Affairs, offer some 33,000 fellowships for study abroad by United States citizens and for study in the United States by citizens of other countries. Many of these are for undergraduate or graduate students, but others, such as the fellowship in Mammalian Biology offered by the San Diego Zoo, and the fellowships in many scientific fields offered by the National Academy of Sciences—National Research Council, are for post-doctoral research workers or even, in some cases, for middle-aged scientists. The number of fellowships available in the National Academy program is unspecified but presumably large, while in others, such as that of the Woman's Auxiliary to the American Society of Mechanical Engineers, only one fellowship is offered.

Other forms of cooperation

Other forms of cooperation include the relatively simultaneous measurement of phenomena that cut across national boundaries or are worldwide in nature. Careful planning, continuous communication, and free exchange of data are essential for success here. The International Geophysical Year, described in some detail below, was an example of this kind of cooperation.

In all fields of science, it has long been recognized that standards of measurement and methods of observation must be inter-calibrated on an international basis. The rise of many new sciences and technologies has multiplied the problem in recent years.

Some experimental instruments, such as the high-energy particle accelerator of modern physics, are not only fantastically expensive but extremely difficult to construct and operate. International cooperation in financing and utilizing accelerators has been quite successful at the European Center for Nuclear Research (CERN), and accelerators in the United States and the U.S.S.R. have also been made available to scientists of various nations.

COOPERATION IN TECHNICAL ASSISTANCE

Technical assistance comprises those measures, short of the provision of significant capital, undertaken by a technically advanced country or intergovernmental organization to develop the human and natural resources and technical capabilities of a less advanced country. The concept in its modern form is only about fifteen years old, though it has roots in colonial and missionary practices. Scientific research and the analytical methods of science have not been used to the maximum in any technical assistance programs, most of which have been in the hands of educators, engineers, and others concerned with short-term goals. Research is generally of limited usefulness in solving short-range problems, though modern methods of analysis of these problems could be better utilized than they have been.

Short-term problems often seem critically important, but the ultimate purpose of technical assistance must be the long-range one of assisting other nations in their economic, political, and social development into free and viable communities in a modern world. For the long run, research can make significant contributions in many areas. Scientific investigation of major problems—both long-standing and emergent—which impede the social and economic growth of developing nations can lead to strengthening the basic resources of a country and its people.

While some technical assistance programs have been notably successful, the results of many have been disappointing. Among the reasons for the limited success of much technical assistance has been lack of knowledge about such factors as the nature of change in societies and its dependence and effects upon individuals and upon the structure and mores of the society; inadequate means for effective communication of skills and ideas between different societies and cultures; and the limited applicability of technologies developed under one set of conditions to markedly different situations.

It has been possible to double the yield of wheat on the large farms of Mexico by using improved seed, chemical fertilizers, and better agricultural practices. But these measures have been relatively ineffective under the conditions of small farm plots and archaic land tenure in Iran. Applied research on the coastal fisheries of Peru, sponsored by the U.N. Special Fund and undertaken by the Food and Agriculture Organization is notably successful. But the attempt to introduce Norwegian scientific fisheries methods off the coast of Kerala in India has been frustrated by the lack of repair facilities for motorized fishing vessels and the difficulties of developing a market for the catch. The Helmand River Dam in Afghanistan is a monument to skilled engineering, but part of the lands brought under irrigation are rapidly deteriorating because of water logging and salination of the soil. Much valuable technical equipment has been distributed to educational institutions in the less developed countries. But a good deal of it no longer works, either because skilled repair and maintenance men are not available or because no one on the staff of the recipient institution has a scientific problem which requires the use of the equipment. Plants for production of antibiotics and other highly technical products have been built in some developing countries, but because they are isolated from an industrial complex and usually operate far below capacity, the cost of production may be as much as ten times as high as that of comparable products in the advanced countries.

In attempting to improve the policies and practices of technical assistance, research and development can enlarge our body of knowledge and skill. The whole spectrum of the natural, social, and behavioral sciences should be utilized to understand the nature of transition in developing areas and to forecast the effectiveness of assistance proposals.

New technologies for the developing countries

Much modern technology must be simplified to be useful to developing countries. New technologies suited to available energy sources, environment, and economic and social patterns must often be developed. To meet the specific needs of particular underdeveloped countries or regions, substantial efforts should also be devoted to devising adaptations from the vast store of modern scientific and technical knowledge. This adaptive research must usually be performed in the area or region concerned. At any rate, the problems must be identified and the proposed solutions must be tested there.

These countries are overwhelmingly rural, and one of their key problems is that of electrical or mechanical energy in the villages. What can modern science and technology offer the villager to lighten his toil and strengthen his hands, within the means he can afford? The diffuseness of the market for energy in the villages makes supply in modern forms a difficult problem.

There are numerous unsolved problems of public health in tropical countries. Radically cheapening the purification of water would be of great benefit. So would simple, culturally acceptable outdoor latrines and indoor toilets not requiring running water. Applications of nutritional knowledge, particularly to the problem of animal protein deficiency in human diets are urgently needed to aid the proper growth of children and improve the vitality of adults. Simple methods of refrigeration for food storage and for cooling of houses would help in nutrition by reducing food wastage. Solar energy research offers intriguing opportunities in this and other connections.

To lift agriculture above the subsistence level, abundant, cheap, and properly regulated water is needed for irrigation. Applied research and development should be conducted on means for location of underground water, drilling and pumping of wells, prevention of evaporation losses in reservoirs and in the farmers' fields, inexpensive lining of irrigation canals to prevent seepage, desalination of water, and higher-yielding, salt-tolerant crops.

In nearly all low-income countries, human population growth is outrunning increases in production. The importance of biological research on inexpensive, effective methods of contraception, and sociological and psychological investigations of the barriers to population control, cannot be over-emphasized.

Some facets of the research needs of the low income countries can be met in the laboratories of the scientifically advanced nations, but most of the research must be done locally in order to meet local conditions. This means that building up of research capacities within the countries is fundamental to any kind of technical progress.

The barriers separating the academic world of more or less "pure" science from the world of everyday action in agriculture, industry, health, and social problems tend to be particularly great in the less developed countries. Their scientists and engineers need the encouragement and example of western colleagues in research collaboration on their urgent applied problems.

University and other sister relationships

One of the most promising organizational patterns by which the scientific research communities of technologically advanced countries can contribute to the progress of newly developing countries is through long-term inter-institutional cooperation.

Such sister relationships need especially to be established between western universities and the universities of the less advanced countries. The relationships should include a systematic interchange of faculty, research staff, and graduate students, joint selection of problems and assignment of priorities for research, searching out and drawing upon existing scientific and technological knowledge, bringing to bear specialized scientific talent and specialized equipment otherwise not available to the newly developing country, and collaboration in methods for bridging the gap between research and practical action.

A successful example of such a relationship is that between the University of California Medical School at San Francisco and two of the medical schools in Indonesia.

A consortium of American technical schools and universities has undertaken to provide long-term help for the new technical institute at Kampur in India. On a smaller scale Washington State University has worked with the Lyallpur Agricultural College in West Pakistan, and Texas A & M College has assisted the engineering university at Dacca in East Pakistan. Many other examples could be given. Similar sister relationships exist among governmental scientific agencies in different countries, such as the one between the United States Geological Survey and the corresponding natural resources agencies in several South American countries.

Development of scientific participation

Advice from scientists experienced in planning and administration is greatly needed by many countries in helping to establish scientific research organizations and research priorities, and in producing scientists. The values and methods of science must be woven into the fabric of any society that is to be viable in the modern world. No country can afford to rely entirely on technical advice from foreign specialists, who are bound to be unfamiliar with its broadest and deepest problems. In our era of revolutionary technical change each country must have its own specialists, who have the sophistication and scientific insight to be able to evaluate the potentialities of technical innovations in the context of their own society. More important, the traditional and static social structures of the less advanced countries must be leavened with the spirit of rational inquiry, the recognition of uncertainty, and the patient, hardworking optimism of science. Finally, no country that fails to contribute at least in a small way to the advance of scientific understanding can in the long run participate fully and with dignity in the economic and social benefits of scientific discovery. Many developing countries recognize these facts and have sought advice in establishing their own programs of scientific research and development.

The developing countries need material assistance as well as advice if they are to participate in modern science. Even in such a relatively advanced country as India, there is a tragic scarcity of scientific books and periodicals, scientific instruments, and biological reference collections. Instruments on hand are often out of service because spare parts are not available. Easily accessible funds for instrument repairs and replacement are of vital importance.

Equally serious in the poorer countries is the lack of jobs—and status —for young scientists. Many of us have helped with the advanced education of young people from these countries who have later reported their lack of opportunity to use their specialized training back at home. Some of them have had to find work entirely outside science simply to keep their families alive.

Foundations or government agencies for the support of free research proposed by scientists themselves, analogous to the National Science Foundation in the United States, exist in few countries. Consequently, young scientists in most regions of the world struggle against great odds in following their own scientific imaginations and insights.

Scientific education

In spite of the present lack of opportunities for work and status for young scientists in many countries, there is, nevertheless, on a world-wide basis a critical shortage both of creative scientists and of technicians to assist them. One answer is to increase the quantity and improve the quality of scientific education at all levels, but particularly in the middle schools and colleges. In many countries, scientific subjects are taught from a syllabus which is not only difficult and dull, but several decades out of date. In some schools in the United States and elsewhere successful changes in scientific teaching have been made. In these new curricula the marvelous advances of the past few decades in mathematics, physics, and chemistry are used to stretch the minds and stir the imaginations of young people, and at the same time accelerate the pace of their scientific education. Some of these new curricula could be adapted to conditions in other countries. Delay in utilizing them seems traceable in part to the conservatism of educators and the slow pace of governments, and in part to failures of communication between scientific educators. International cooperation in developing methods of scientific education is very much needed.

MECHANISMS OF INTERNATIONAL SCIENTIFIC COOPERATION

The simplest and perhaps the best mechanism of international cooperation in science involves two or three scientists from different countries working together in the same laboratory on a common problem. Often one is a teacher, the others his pupils. But in science all are equals; ideas and insights more often than not come from the pupils.

Many more formal means of scientific cooperation exist, varying widely in complexity and effectiveness—generally in inverse ratio.

For many years, private scientific and philanthropic foundations have played a major role in international scientific cooperation. During the last fifteen years their activities have been overshadowed by the larger-scale operations of governments, but the effectiveness of the foundations per unit of money or effort still ranks very high, because of their sophistication and experience.

The principal international organizations of scientists themselves are the 13 great international unions and their coordinating body, the International Council of Scientific Unions (ICSU). The unions are very effective in fostering scientific communications through congresses and symposia, but they have proved singularly ineffective in cooperative research programs. Consequently, the Council has developed a new device: the special committee consisting of a small group of scientists drawn from the unions and operating through national committees in the cooperating countries. The International Geophysical Year was an outstanding example of a cooperative research program carried through by a special committee.

The International Council is now in a critical stage, largely because of the increasing recognition by governments of the importance of international science and their consequent desire to control it. In the future, ICSU may be managed by the national academies of different countries, which are usually fairly responsive to their own governments, rather than, as at present, by the international unions, which are autonomous, self-perpetuating bodies of scientists.

A few regional scientific organizations, such as the Pacific Science Association and the Pan Indian Ocean Science Association, have been effective in fostering international scientific communication, at least in certain fields. However, these organizations have been even less effective than the international unions in developing programs of cooperative research.

A great many intergovernmental organizations have undertaken responsibilities for international scientific cooperation. Some, such as the World Meteorological Organization, the International Atomic Energy Agency, and the new Intergovernmental Oceanographic Commission, are concerned exclusively with science and technology. Others, such as UNESCO, the World Health Organization, and the Food and Agriculture Organization, have broad missions which include scientific as well as other activities. All suffer from an inadequate budget, ponderous administrative machinery, and insufficient technical staff. Nevertheless, they thoroughly justify themselves as essential components of international scientific action. If they did not already exist it would be necessary to invent them.

Some regional intergovernmental organizations such as the International Council for the Exploration of the Sea, the European Center for Nuclear Research, and the Inter-American Tropical Tuna Commission have very effectively advanced scientific research on an international scale. Others, such as the Organization of American States, have as yet had little impact on science.

BARRIERS TO COOPERATION

Many kinds of national barriers interfere with the freedom and advance of science. They include economic restrictions on the passage of instruments across national boundaries; passport and visa restrictions which often involve conference-killing delays; and restrictions on the geographical areas of operation of research craft and scientific exploring parties. Since all these barriers involve the policies of governments, interactions between the scientific community in each country and its government, and between the international scientific community and the various intergovernmental organizations are needed to reduce or remove the obstacles.

Visa and immigration barriers

Since the early 1950's, the problems of visas and immigration restrictions for foreign scientists coming to the United States have been considerably eased, not by legislation but through administrative action by the State Department and the Immigration Service. Applicants for a visa no longer need to fill out complicated and puzzling questionnaires, and they are no longer fingerprinted. For most applicants, non-immigrant "visitor" visas are now issued by larger United States Consular posts in less than an hour's time on the first visit. In nearly all cases, visitors armed with a visa are passed by the Immigration Service, even though the applicant has to meet the same tests at the port of entry that he met when applying for a visa, and the Immigration Officer's determination is independent of that of the Consular Officer.

The law prohibits the issuance of a visa on some 30 different grounds, including past or present membership in proscribed organizations or advocacy of subversive doctrines. Legally the Consular Officer on the spot has the final authority to decide whether a visa shall be issued, and his decision is not subject to any judicial or administrative review whatsoever. In present practice, however, Consular Officers refer most doubtful cases to the State Department and the Attorney General, who can and usually do waive most of the grounds of ineligibility if the applicant is coming for a temporary visit.

During the 1950's it was almost impossible to hold an international scientific conference in the United States because of the difficulties of getting many prominent scientists through the visa and immigration barriers. Under the law, a scientist from one of the Iron Curtain countries is almost certain to be ineligible for a visa, both because he belongs to proscribed organizations and because he is liable to advocate subversive doctrines. The State Department and the Attorney General, by using their discretionary authority, now usually admit scientists from most of these countries, and the problem ordinarily resolves itself into getting the visas issued before the conference is over. Many a conference organizer has suffered a mild neurosis in his attempts to quicken the stately pace of the State Department. It is still very difficult to get scientists from some countries through the barriers. These are the countries which the State Department does not recognize, such as mainland China, or which in its view do not exist, such as East Germany.

Removal of barriers by intergovernmental action

Two examples of recent intergovernmental actions to facilitate scientific research are the Treaty on Antarctica and the International Convention on the Scientific Exploration of the Continental Shelf. In the Antarctic Treaty the entire continent has been set aside as a theatre for scientific research and exploration, and all the signatory countries have agreed to waive any claims to Antarctic territory for the next 50 years. The Convention on the Continental Shelf provides that scientific research in the shallow coastal areas outside territorial waters can be conducted by scientists of any country, provided the research culminates in open publication and scientists from the coastal state are allowed to participate. The coastal state must give its permission for such research, but the Convention provides that "this permission will not ordinarily be refused." Unfortunately the Convention has not yet come into force because it has not been ratified by a sufficient number of States.

An increasingly serious barrier to research in the fields of radio-astronomy, space science, oceanography, and meteorology is the commercial pre-emption of radio frequencies for television and communications. Although no definite solutions are yet in sight, the International Council of Scientific Unions has taken vigorous steps to ensure the allotment of critically important frequencies for radio-astronomy and to reduce interference on other frequency bands used for scientific purposes.

The International Geophysical Year

By far the largest, most complex, and most expensive enterprise ever undertaken in international scientific cooperation was the International Geophysical Year. The IGY involved about 60,000 scientists and technicians from 66 nations working at thousands of stations literally from pole to pole. No one has ventured to estimate the total cost, but it was certainly in excess of a billion dollars. This vast and daring enterprise caught the imagination of the world and gave men everywhere a new conception of their planetary home. It helped to construct scientific bridges across political chasms, and greatly increased the role of science and of scientists in national policy-making and in diplomacy. Much solid scientific accomplishment also came out of the IGY.

The joint assault on Antarctica by some thirteen nations gave us a new level of knowledge about the shape and topography of that ice-buried continent. Coordinated studies of particles from the sun and their effects on the earth's upper atmosphere and surrounding plasma were made possible by the elaborate planning and communications systems developed during the IGY. New impetus was given to seismology and the study of the earth's interior. In oceanography, much was learned about the ocean currents deep beneath the surface of the sea, and about the shape and structure of the deep sea floor. The great adventure of our time, man's exploration of outer space, began during the IGY, and was undoubtedly accelerated by it.

But perhaps of equal importance for the future was the IGY discovery of a most effective means of international scientific cooperation. Nearly all the money spent during the IGY was spent by each nation separately in support of its own scientists who were taking part in the international program. Only a few hundred thousand dollars were required for the apparatus of international coordination. Committees of scientists in each of the countries developed their own programs, and these were presented to scientists of the other countries in a series of international meetings where programs were compared and plans for extensive modifications—usually expansions—were made. Scientists of each country would then return home and put pressure on their government to provide financial support for the national program developed in the conference, basing their arguments largely on national prestige, on "keeping up with the Joneses." Thus the great enterprise grew by a series of bootstrap-lifting stages.

Another long-range benefit of the IGY was its development of mechanisms for exchange of scientific data. World data centers were established in the United States, the U.S.S.R., and in Europe, and elaborate agreements were entered into by the scientists of the participating countries to provide each of these centers with all of the measurements made under the different scientific programs. As far as is known, these agreements were fairly well kept.

The peculiar virtues of the IGY centered on avoidance of a ponderous international bureaucracy; planning in each country by the scientists directly involved—an arrangement which led to a liberal interpretation of the objectives and scope of the scientific work eligible for support under the IGY umbrella; development of a means for large-scale support by individual governments; and development of mechanisms for free exchange of a wide variety of scientific data.

But the IGY had defects as well as virtues: the emphasis was inevitably on systematic collection of relatively routine observations rather than on the individual theoretical and experimental work which constitutes the chief means of progress in scientific understanding. The whole enterprise was a high-pressure affair, and consequently its cost, in terms of human effort, as well as money, was perhaps excessive relative to the results obtained. Political considerations intruded themselves to the extent that the great land mass of mainland China was blanked out in the international program of observations. At least in certain fields, the scientific representatives of some countries at the international planning conferences had no real authority to agree to any modifications of their national programs. Hence, there was far less coordination of the actual scientific work than would have been desirable.

COOPERATION IN OUTER SPACE

At the initiative of the United States, the United Nations General Assembly recently took a first step toward international cooperation in outer space. The Assembly resolution called for a regime of law in human space activities; promotion of scientific cooperation and exchange of information about results obtained in astrophysical and geophysical research; a worldwide undertaking in weather forecasting and weather research; and international cooperation in the establishment of a global system of communication satellites. Under the terms of the resolution, outer space and celestial bodies, like the high seas and Antarctica, are free for exploration by all states in conformity with international law, and are not subject to appropriation.

One measure of information exchange is already under way: a comprehensive public registry of all objects launched into orbit or beyond. The space powers are being asked to submit information on a voluntary basis about their national programs.

Cooperation in space research

A proposal has been made to construct, at a location near the Equator, an international sounding rocket facility under United Nations auspices. The government of India has expressed interest in having this joint venture of the United Nations located on its territory. Such a launching base for scientific rockets would be of great value in exploring the peculiar phenomena of the high upper atmosphere which exist in the neighborhood of the Equator, and in some unknown way are related to the rotation of the earth.

The United States and Russia have discussed a number of scientific projects in which cooperation between the two countries might be desirable, including mapping of the earth's magnetic field, research in the medical aspects of manned space flights, and cooperative studies of Mars and Venus. Under United Nations auspices, these bilateral projects could become multilateral undertakings with wider participation.

Weather forecasting and research

The third part of the U.N. space program looks toward worldwide weather forecasting and meteorological research. Orbiting weather satellites, supplementing other advances in meteorological technology, such as sounding rockets, radar, and electronic computers, will make it possible for the first time to observe continuously the entire atmosphere of the earth. The World Meteorological Organization (WMO) has been asked to develop an international weather service—a global network to receive, process, and transmit meteorological information from weather satellites as well as from earth-based instruments. First steps would include the establishment of three world weather centers for the collection and dissemination of data in Washington, Moscow, and a city in the Southern Hemisphere; the establishment of regional centers; and the filling of existing gaps in the global network of ground and ship observatories. The United States is already making available to other countries the information received from its Tiros satellites. As a result of recent bilateral discussions between American and Russian space officials, it is hoped that the Soviet Union will soon follow suit with its own weather satellites.

In the long run, international cooperation in meteorological research may be more important than this development of meteorological services. To explore these possibilities, a collaborative effort is needed between the World Meteorological Organization and UNESCO, based on the proposals of the private scientific community operating through the International Council of Scientific Unions. In the words of a recent WMO report, "It is not unrealistic to expect that mankind will eventually have the power to influence weather and even climate on a large scale." By encouraging cooperation now, we may reduce the risk that this power will eventually be used by one nation to achieve military or economic advantage at the expense of others.

Space communications

The fourth part of the U.N. program of space cooperation looks toward the establishment of a global system of communication satellites.

With the aid of satellites, telephone communication between continents will be immeasurably easier. Twenty times the number of telephone channels in our existing undersea cables will become available. If intercontinental telephone communication increases sufficiently to fill this huge capacity, it may someday be possible to place a call to any place in the world for approximately the same charge as to another city in the United States.

The satellite system likely to be in use within this decade will be a point-to-point relay between central installations in different countries. This means that the benefits of space communication can be provided for all peoples only through political as well as technical cooperation. The U.N. resolution has stated the principle that satellite communication should be developed as soon as practicable on a global and non-discriminatory basis. Efforts should be made to establish a single system for all nations of the world, rather than competing systems between contending political blocs.

Like the World Meteorological Organization in the weather field, the International Telecommunications Union has been asked by the General Assembly to report on ways of promoting cooperation in space communications. In October 1963, it will hold a special conference to allocate radio frequencies for use in outer space, including those needed for communication satellite systems. Agreement on the reservation of an adequate part of the limited radio frequency spectrum for space communication, and the establishment of ground rules which will assure non-interference of space communications of different countries with each other, or with other services on the earth, is an obvious prerequisite to further action.

The establishment of global satellite communications will require international agreement on many questions, such as the choice of the system to be used, participation in ownership of the system, allocation of satellite channels between uses and users, location of ground terminals, technical standardization, assistance to less developed countries, and rates to be charged for different services. Although many of these questions are analogous to those that have been solved in conventional communications systems, others raise new and unprecedented problems.

Upper and lower limits of space cooperation

At present, the deep political differences of our time place an upper limit on space cooperation. Messrs. Glenn and Titov will probably not ride to the moon on the same space ship. But there is, or should be, also a lower limit to this cooperation, if the nations can take a realistic view of their own self-interests. All countries, whatever their ideology, can agree that space and celestial bodies should not be the subject of competing national claims, that cooperative experiments should be undertaken and information exchanged, that worldwide weather services should be developed, and that communications among nations should be improved.

The National Aeronautics and Space Administration already has cooperative ventures with some forty countries, involving tracking stations, exchanges of personnel, and joint space experiments. For certain countries, and for certain activities, cooperative projects may be easier of achievement if they are multilateral and bear United Nations endorsement.

THE FEDERAL GOVERNMENT

The importance of the scientific health of the country, the relationship between science and national strength and security, and the increasing magnitude of the cost of research, have led to general acceptance of the idea that financial support for science in the United States is a necessary function of the federal government.

As the Government has expanded its involvement, it has found itself engaged to an ever-increasing extent in international scientific activities. It has sponsored international scientific expeditions, enabled American scientists to participate in international conferences (and even helped support their international organizations), brought foreign scientists to the United States, cooperated with other nations in mounting experiments, and enlisted the scientific resources of friendly countries where our own resources were inadequate.

Other considerations beyond the scientific have been important factors in the international scientific activities of the Government: the research potential of our allies needed rebuilding if they were to become once again strong economically and militarily; our efforts to aid the less-developed countries call for scientific and technological as well as economic assistance; the conduct of research on a cooperative basis and the relationships established in the international scientific community can be used as political instruments, common objectives can be developed with other nations and meaningful contacts can be made among influential groups in alien societies.

Broader objectives are also involved, though they are rarely stated explicitly because of the need to justify expenditures by direct self-interest. The advancement of science for human welfare is one of these; another is the conviction that science is a common intellectual activity of mankind and hence its worldwide health and vigor are legitimate concerns of this nation.

Federal scientific activities overseas have grown in large part through the action of individual agencies which have seen a need in the light of their own missions. This is the historical course of development of United States government activities.

Support of research by foreign scientists overseas

One of the international aspects of the federal involvement in science is support of the research of foreign scientists overseas. It may be used as an example of the more general problems of governmental action in international science. This support has been growing steadily since it was begun in Europe by the American military following World War II; in fiscal year 1962 it was on the order of $25-30 million. Active programs are conducted by at least five major government departments and agencies. The Department of Health, Education and Welfare, for example, went from expenditures of $100,000 in 1955 to $8 million in 1961, and to an anticipated $12 million in 1962. The program of the Department of Agriculture has fluctuated widely, being some $3.5 million in 1960, $33.5

million in 1961, and $5 million in 1962, the fluctuations being due in part to changes in policy with respect to use of foreign currency. In several advanced countries the money available for research in some fields from United States government sources is more than the funds available from within the country.

The bulk of the United States overseas research support programs have been justified as being necessary, or at least useful, in the light of the missions of particular agencies. Most agencies, when providing support, have selected foreign scientists who have some special capabilities in terms of location, competence, or facilities. The Department of Defense modifies this "uniqueness" criterion. The military interests of the United States are served by broadening their scientific base with the ideas that flow from close relationships with good scientists wherever they may be located.

In the less-advanced countries, we have supported research in order to assist economic development, as well as for its own sake. Here, the number of capable scientists is much smaller than in the advanced countries, and the local governments are often unable to provide adequate support. As a result, United States assistance to individual institutions or scientists has a far-reaching impact on the scientific life of the country.

In some of these countries, foreign currency surpluses earned through the sale of United States agricultural commodities (PL-480 Funds) are used to finance the research. Apparently as an accident of administrative agreement, the support of research is given a lower priority than other uses to which the PL-480 funds may be put. The result is that local currency is available for research only when all other needs have been satisfied. The funds in local currency could often be usefully salted with small amounts of dollar funds for purchase of equipment and scientific journals, and for travel.

Concentration on supporting research overseas related to the missions of United States agencies leaves many gaps where, for a mixture of scientific and foreign policy purposes, the United States government should be active. Support related to foreign aid can be budgeted through the Agency for International Development, but there are other situations where technical assistance is not involved and the research program is not strictly within agency missions, yet should be supported.

At present, there is no ready means to carry out overseas research support programs, or other scientific activities, when they are clearly justified for foreign policy reasons and represent good science, but may not fall within the purview of a single agency's mission. The National Science Foundation is the only federal agency charged with looking after the health of United States science as a whole. The Foundation should be given the authority to request funds for international activities, such as the support of certain kinds of research abroad, that fall in the grey area of mixed scientific and foreign policy objectives.

Other agencies, such as Agriculture, Health, Education and Welfare, and Interior, that are working in fields directly related to human welfare, should be given limited responsibility to support basic research that furthers their fields of emphasis, whether or not the practical application of the research is tied to a problem encountered in the United States. Particularly in the PL-480 program, the restriction of pertinency to a United States domestic problem could be removed without raising administrative difficulties.

As federal programs of support of research by foreign scientists have grown in size and proliferated in numbers, concerns have arisen that they may no longer serve some of the broader objectives of United States policy or may actually be in opposition to them.

In the early days of United States support in Europe, our programs were an important factor in many countries in increasing their awareness of the values and usefulness of science, thereby increasing the level of domestic support provided for research. In some countries our support helped to keep good scientists productive, and prevented frustration during a period when the local government was unable to provide full support itself. Our assistance encouraged scientists to remain in their native lands, rather than migrate to the United States or elsewhere in the hope of finding support for their work. Scientists working on United States grants or contracts were able to visit the United States and thereby to increase face-to-face scientific communication. American support helped to identify and support promising younger scientists, and enable outstanding university teachers to take responsibility for more graduate students. These programs also demonstrated that governments can support science across national borders effectively, and, to a measure, disinterestedly for the good of all men and nations. The patterns thus begun may prove to be of great and lasting value.

As a result of the rapidly advancing European economic situation, some of these programs may now be working against full assumption of responsibility for research support by local governments. Our objectives should lead us in a different direction—to emphasis on cooperative research. Cooperation can be multilateral or bilateral, but it should involve investment by all parties concerned. European and American scientists should be encouraged to plan projects jointly and to submit a joint proposal to both governments. This is actually being done in the development of a bilateral program of cooperation between United States and Japanese scientists, sponsored jointly in this country by the State Department and the National Science Foundation.

Joint planning and submission of proposals does not happen automatically; the research-supporting agencies need actively to encourage such planning and to provide support for necessary travel and meetings. The National Aeronautics and Space Administration in its overseas programs has insisted on local support for cooperative projects.

There are also some dangers in supporting research in the less advanced countries. One is that of unintentionally impeding the development of a country rather than contributing to it. In supporting research by individual scientists on problems of interest to United States agencies, we may keep them from teaching or from other work that should have priority. In India, for example, there is apparently some feeling that the availability of United States support encourages more people to devote themselves to basic research than the country can afford. Whatever the merits of this concern in particular cases, the United States government, and particularly the Department of State, must be in a better position than it is now to evaluate local situations, to monitor programs, and to establish policy direction on a country or regional basis. Particular care needs to be exercised in furnishing support through military agencies. In some countries it may be unfortunate, in terms of our other objectives, if the United States presents the appearance that it is primarily for military purposes that the government supports science.

Strengthening the role of the State Department

United States government participation in international scientific activities appears to be based on four principles:

1. To advance science in the United States it is necessary to encourage wide contacts between American and foreign scientists, engage in international scientific ventures, and often support scientists in other countries in their research;

2. To support our military effort and our general security objectives, it is essential to ensure a strong scientific base in allied countries and utilize scientific competence wherever it exists;

3. To support our foreign policy objectives, it is important to encourage international scientific contacts and activities. By this means we foster acceptance of the Western intellectual tradition, establish relationships with intellectual groups in the communist world, develop common goals and objectives with other nations, strengthen international organizations, enhance the scientific image of the United States, and assist the growth of the less-developed countries;

4. The advancement of science in all nations contributes to man's intellectual and material well-being, and hence aids in achieving the long-term goals of the United States.

International scientific activities have come to have an important relation to United States objectives in other fields, and hence require well-formulated and clearly understood policy guidance, and integration overseas on a continuing basis with other aspects of United States foreign policy. The beginnings of the necessary mechanisms exist but need strengthening. In Washington, the Office of the Science Adviser in the

Department of State has already been enlarged and upgraded in the Departmental hierarchy, to be able more effectively to meet the present-day requirements of establishing a foreign policy for science and of integrating scientific factors into foreign policy formulation. According to the Department's announcement, the Director of the new Office of International Scientific Affairs will be a Principal Officer of the Department with rank administratively equivalent to a bureau head. He will serve as adviser to the Secretary and provide advice to the Department and the Foreign Service on scientific and technological matters, and will direct the work of the Office of International Scientific Affairs which will have bureau status. The functions of the office have been expanded to include cognizance of the peaceful uses of outer space and atomic energy, which were previously handled separately.

A more effective mechanism is also required overseas to provide information, evaluate the situation in each country, recommend policy and program changes, and implement policy decisions. This could be accomplished through strengthened and expanded science attaché programs, particularly in those countries or regions in which there are extensive United States scientific activities. During the last two years the number of Science Attachés serving at overseas posts has increased to 17. Today the following posts have one or two attachés: London (2), Paris (2), Bonn (2), Stockholm (2), Rome (2), New Delhi (2), Tokyo (2), Buenos Aires (1), Bern (1), Rio de Janeiro (1). The post at Rio is a regional office for Latin America with science representation from the National Institutes of Health, the National Science Foundation, and the Department of Defense.

SOME LIABILITIES

Far-reaching advances in science have usually come from individual scientists or groups of scientists doing what they are interested in at the moment, freely and excitedly following up new observations or insights in an essentially anarchic and unplanned fashion. The cumbersome apparatus of planning, logistics, agreement, and direction essential for cooperative international research is anathema to this kind of science.

In general the planning and direction of international scientific action is done either by bureaucrats or by so-called scientific statesmen, usually men who have long since ceased to do significant scientific research. Science is a young man's game, and the young giants who are the real creators need to be brought in. But often they are too busy with their own research to be bothered with how other people should do theirs.

Science has become so expensive and so important that it can only be supported financially by governments, but there is still in all countries, even the most advanced ones, a profound lack of understanding of science by politicians, a situation often matched by the equally profound mis-understanding of politics by scientists. By its very nature, science is more concerned with understanding than with action; politics can deal only with action and must attack today's problems regardless of the long future. Since governments tend to regard science as only one among many tools to be used in the accomplishment of social, economic, foreign policy, or military missions, they do not hesitate to restrict or impede it to serve short-range goals. The concept of science for its own sake of gaining understanding—because understanding is a natural right of human beings—has never been more than partially accepted by politicians. Progress toward true international free-masonry of science must neces-sarily be slow.

THE CHALLENGE OF THE FUTURE

In the past, international scientific cooperation has been most success-ful when it has dealt with the problems of communication among scientists, with removal of the barriers to scientific research, or with other matters regarding what might be called the internal business of science. But there are many problems of tragic intensity and worldwide scope facing modern man: the wise use of the earth's resources; the rational control of the sizes of human populations; the great disparity in the levels of nutrition and the incidence of disease between peoples; and the problem of arms control. It is by no means clear how scientific coopera-tion on a worldwide basis can best be used to attack these appalling questions of our time. But it is obvious that their solutions will be found only if science and technology are brought to bear in the broadest possi-ble way and with urgent intensity.

Philip H. Coombs

5

The Past and Future in Perspective

In the hope of seeing more clearly where we have been, where we are, and, especially, where we should go from here, this closing chapter views through a wide-angle lens the broad direction and shape of our national effort in the field of international educational, scientific and cultural affairs.

The future poses many difficult questions which must be grappled with even though we cannot hope to emerge with final answers and tidy blueprints. For example: what role and importance should these activities be given in the conduct of United States foreign policy? What specific guidelines to policy and action should be pursued? What practical steps should be taken to fill important gaps and to increase the effectiveness of our present effort? What should be the magnitude of our national effort and how should it be financed? How should this effort be organized and better unified? And what is the best division of labor between federal, private, and international agencies?

Questions such as these have fortunately been given thoughtful study in recent months and years by a variety of able people. It is encouraging that their conclusions, though reached from many different starting points, are in substantial harmony and reflect an emerging national consensus among experts on "where we should go from here."

But agreeing on where to go is only part of the problem. Finding a way

In 1961-1962 Philip H. Coombs *was Assistant Secretary of State for Educational and Cultural Affairs. Before that he was with The Ford Foundation as Program Director for Education. A former professor of economics at Amherst, Dr. Coombs has been economics advisor to the Governor of Connecticut and executive director of the Paley Commission. He has also been consultant on education to foreign governments and a member or chairman of United States delegations to international conferences—among them the "Alliance for Progress" conference and the United States-Japanese Cultural Conference. He has written widely on cultural aspects of foreign policy. He is now with the Brookings Institution in Washington, D. C.*

to get there, to translate good ideas into practical action, is often more difficult. Yet even here it may be illuminating to begin with an examination of our past experience.

FROM CULTURAL IMPORTER TO EXPORTER

With all the talk these days about American foreign aid, we sometimes forget that for a very long time the shoe was on the other foot. For its first 150 years, roughly up to World War II, the United States was a major recipient of foreign assistance, though not so labeled. In the broadest sense of "culture" we were a large cultural importer and a minor exporter. We drew enormous strength for all aspects of our development from the cultural resources of the Old World—its educational and political institutions, its storehouse of knowledge, literature, music and art, its technology and brainpower.

Had we followed a national policy of isolationism and protectionism in the cultural field as we did in international politics and economics, we would not be the leader of the free world today. From the outset the United States has thrived on the benefits of a "cultural common market" which embraced most of the western world.

Our educational system is a case in point. As Howard Wilson noted earlier, it is an amalgam of imported and homegrown ingredients. The kindergarten and the Ph.D. came from Germany, the grade school and liberal arts college from England, and we invented for ourselves the junior high, the comprehensive high school, and the land grant college. A complete carbon copy of another nation's educational system would not have suited our needs, but we were able to make good use of some imported parts. (This is well to remember whenever we are tempted, as we sometimes are, to "sell" our educational system—lock, stock and barrel —to the developing countries of today.)

It is significant to our present analysis that up to 15 years ago the United States government had almost nothing to do with this beneficial cultural traffic that richly nourished our social, political, and economic development—except to stand aside and let it happen. There was no public policy and no government program in this realm of our foreign relations; it remained the almost exclusive domain of private laissez-faire, and still does to a high degree.

Since the Second World War the situation has shifted drastically. The United States has now become the world's largest cultural exporter, though we continue to be a large cultural importer, larger than ever (which is how to sustain our vigor). And the government has now entered the field with a myriad of official programs.

One good illustration of our changed "cultural trade" position is the two-way flow of foreign students. For many generations American students journeyed to the great universities and scientific and medical institutes of Europe, from which they returned to become teachers, research scholars, and builders of American institutions. Today our students continue to study abroad, in much larger numbers than before, but the difference is that now we receive three times as many students from other countries as we send abroad, three quarters of them from the developing nations of Asia, Africa, the Near and Middle East, and Latin America. What they take home is an American "cultural export"; and what they teach us is a "cultural import."

Students, however, are only one element, though a very important one, in our expanded cultural trade. The book and magazine, the film and musical recording, radio, television and now Telstar, the visiting professor and specialist, the tourist and merchant, the soldier and seaman, the performing artist and visiting athlete, the adaptation of American institutions, science, and technology to foreign needs—all these are purveyors of cultural influences.

With modern means of communication and travel, these influences move with astonishing speed and range. "The Twist," originating in New York, was being danced by Hong Kong teenagers even before many American parents knew of its existence.

We need not here discuss the causes of our becoming a major cultural exporter, except to emphasize again that it was not the result of conscious public policy. André Malraux observed on a recent visit here that the United States was the first nation in history to become a dominant world power—culturally, politically, and economically—without design, without force, and without intent to conquer or colonize.

Yet, willy-nilly, "the American culture" is spreading rapidly all over the world. Wherever an American travels he finds few things more striking, more bewildering and at times more horrifying, than the conspicuous and ubiquitous impact of "American culture." The variety and contrasts are dramatic. The American University at Beirut, for example, has contributed much to the leadership and modernization of the Arab world and produced many fast friends for the United States. At the same time, the American automobile has brought more traffic problems and a higher fatality rate to Beirut than to Chicago. Many young Latin Americans are wildly enthusiastic about William Faulkner's writing, but their local stores are stocked with lurid paperbacks "Made in the U.S.A." The Indians received Martha Graham's modern dance troupe with great acclaim, but regularly come in droves to view our gangster films.

Returned "Fulbrighters" in Thailand can be observed effectively teaching English and building their nation's school system, with help from our aid mission and Peace Corps volunteers. In contrast one encounters a bitter young Formosan who can find no way to apply at home the advanced scientific training he received in the United States.

Many Indonesian students, as our Attorney General found, are disturbingly ignorant of the liberal progress our nation has made and are easy prey for Marxist distortions. But on the encouraging side, many young Indonesian leaders are more familiar than most Americans with Jefferson's writings, and Chester Bowles' *New Dimensions of Peace* is a worldwide best seller.

In short, American culture today—in all its varied forms, high and low, good and bad—is like a genie loose from the bottle. For better or for worse it is permeating and influencing virtually every other society in the world. These American cultural "exports"—our political and educational philosophy, our technologies and art forms, our language, our fun and games, the examples of our economic progress—along with similar influences from elsewhere in the democratic West, are more responsible for today's worldwide revolution of economic, social, and political systems than the writings of Karl Marx or the maneuvers of the communist nations.

Adoption by other peoples of assorted American cultural fragments, however, does not necessarily give them a balanced understanding, respect, or sympathy for the American society from which the fragments come. Indeed it may even reinforce an already distorted view of our society. Much depends upon how these cultural exports are transmitted and how representative, revealing, and useful they are. But whether they are frivolous or profound, expressions of our best or of our worst, it is clear that they do constitute a powerful force which is reshaping old cultures and the daily lives of other peoples, and molding their attitudes toward the United States and its policies.

Our foreign policy officers, therefore, can no longer ignore or take a light view of these matters. They clearly have fundamental importance to our international relations, to the long-run welfare of this nation and others, and to the prospects for freedom in the world.

POSTWAR PROLIFERATION

The United States was last among the great powers to recognize that educational and cultural affairs have an important role to play in foreign policy, and even yet this recognition is far from adequate.

Our government's first substantial venture into this realm, as we have seen, did not occur until just before the Second World War, largely as a counter-measure to Nazi efforts to penetrate and propagandize Latin America through educational and cultural means. After the war educational and cultural affairs were important in the Allied "reorientation" programs aimed at democratizing defeated Japan and Germany. But these war-connected activities were temporary expedients. They did not represent a commitment to a continuing national policy of giving educational and cultural affairs an important place in our foreign relations, though they helped pave the way.

The real beginning of such a commitment was in 1946 when the United States sponsored the founding of UNESCO and Congress enacted the far-seeing "Fulbright Amendment." These actions opened a new era in our cultural relations with the world. They set us on the road, more by accident than design, toward a national policy that would treat educational and cultural affairs not as a temporary expedient for war but as a major element in a continuing strategy for peace. The timing was fortunate, as it turned out, for there was an imperative though underappreciated need just then for action on the international education fronts.

The United States emerged from the Second World War into a world destined to change more in a single generation than in any previous hundred years, and into a role of leadership for which we were seriously ill-equipped—psychologically, educationally, and by experience. Our tradition of isolation and our western-oriented schools and colleges had not equipped us for this radically altered situation. Our national stockpile of knowledge and experts and our understanding of world affairs were dangerously deficient. Many Americans were acquainted with Europe, but Africa, Latin America, and Asia, even to most teachers and professors, were unfamiliar blotches on the globe. If we were to lead, or even survive, we had much to learn about the diverse peoples of the world—their geography, history, economics, languages, political institutions, and social mores, attitudes and value systems, and most of all about the responsible exercise of international leadership.

But if the United States knew too little about others and was ill-equipped to lead, the rest of the world was almost equally ignorant of us, and unprepared to follow. It was essential that they come quickly to understand our basic goals and the compatibility of these with their own goals and aspirations.

In short, all nations had much to learn about one another, and many misconceptions and hostilities to shed, if the peaceful goals of the new United Nations Charter and of American foreign policy were to have a chance of success. This learning was going to take time, and time would not wait. Meanwhile, the whole world would have to skate for years on dangerously thin ice.

Federal programs

On its 15th birthday in 1961, President Kennedy called the Fulbright Program "the classic modern example of beating swords into plowshares." By then a total of 80,000 American and foreign students, professors, leaders and specialists, had been exchanged with more than 100 countries under the Fulbright and Smith-Mundt programs.

But for all its virtue the early Fulbright Law had serious limitations. It applied only to academic exchanges and then only to countries (largely European) where the United States held foreign currencies derived from war surplus sales. These limitations were broadened considerably in 1948 by passage of the United States Information and Educational Exchange Act (The Smith-Mundt Act) which applied worldwide, authorized dollar appropriations, and provided a broader charter "to cooperate with other nations in the interchange of persons, knowledge and skills; the rendering of technical and other services; the interchange of developments in the field of education, the arts and sciences."

It seems fair to say, however, that in voting for the Smith-Mundt Act, with the "Cold War" now in full swing, most Congressmen were less interested in expanding the two way educational and cultural interchange initiated by the Fulbright Act than in laying firm foundations for a United States overseas information program aimed at countering the vigorous propaganda efforts of the Soviet Bloc. In the late Forties and throughout the Fifties the chief emphasis was on "a campaign of truth," "programs of persuasion," and "psychological strategy," with educational and cultural exchanges taking a back seat to the "fast media."

Later legislative actions broadened the financial base of the Fulbright and Smith-Mundt programs by authorizing the use of payments due the United States from certain other countries (e.g. Finnish War debt and Indian wheat loan payments) and of foreign currencies received from the sale of agricultural surpluses under the Agricultural Trade Development and Assistance Act ("P.L. 480" in 1954). While these foreign currencies permitted an expansion of programs with certain countries, they had the net effect of distorting the worldwide geographical pattern of the exchange program to fit the fortuitous availability of foreign currencies rather than the rapidly evolving obligations, needs and opportunities of the United States. The conspicuous weakness of the State Department's exchange programs in relation to Africa and Latin America in recent years, despite the growing urgency of strengthening our ties with these areas, is largely explained by the scarcity of United States-owned foreign currencies there and the insufficiency of appropriated dollars. The regular dollar appropriations for the Fulbright and Smith-Mundt exchange programs (as distinct from "information" programs) declined from $16 million in 1951 to $14.6 million in 1958, while the number of participating countries rose from 62 to 87.

Another important dimension was added to the State Department's exchange program in 1955 and 1956, largely in response to the rapidly mounting Soviet cultural offensive. The erratic and often poor representation of the United States at international festivals of the performing arts, in contrast to the serious efforts of the Soviet Union, tended to reinforce the widely held and carefully nurtured view that the United States was a nation of materialistic, gadget-happy dollar lovers, devoid of artistic creativity or good taste. To counter this impression the President's Special Program of "cultural presentations" was launched in 1955, using White House funds temporarily to assist a variety of private American performing groups to defray the costs of overseas travel. The following year Congress provided permanent legislative authority for support of such presentations, which subsequently ran the gamut from the Boston, New York and Philadelphia Symphonies, the American Ballet Theatre and the Theatre Guild repertory group starring Helen Hayes, to Hal Holbrook playing Mark Twain, Louis Armstrong playing Africa, and American Olympic athletes playing the field.

Overseas reports from Americans and foreigners alike left no doubt that the impact of these "cultural presentations" on local audiences was highly favorable to the United States. But the very word "culture" remained anathema to certain key members of Congressional appropriations committees who tended to equate it with toe-dancing and wondered how all this could protect foreign countries from communist influence. In any event, the "cultural presentations program" has annually provided a sprightly conversation piece at appropriations time and is an easy mark for all critics, not only those "hard-headed" Congressmen and columnists who are basically unsympathetic to the whole idea, but also those well-meaning private critics who are more sophisticated in the world of performing arts than in the world of practical politics and government operations.

Still another important dimension was added in 1958, this time not in competition but in cooperation with the Soviet Union. The signing of the first US-USSR cultural agreement opened the way to broader contacts with the communist nations of Eastern Europe. This was a major breakthrough for cultural interchange, given the political sensitivities on both sides—the deep reluctance of the Soviet leaders to expose their people to Western influences and the popular fear in the United States that anyone visiting Russia or even learning the language might somehow be subverted. The agreement involved exchanging a variety of students, scholars, technicians, performing artists, books, magazines, and films on a strictly reciprocal basis, which resulted in a cumbersome and sometimes ludicrous diplomatic game of tit-for-tat.

In retrospect, however, what is surprising is not that there have been many sticky problems but that this Soviet exchange has worked so well. When the time for renewal of the agreement arrived in 1961, both governments readily agreed that it should be extended and somewhat enlarged, suggesting that both sides saw advantage in the arrangement. Though the negotiations as usual were long and drawn out, they were harmonious (despite the concurrent issue of West Berlin) and they did end successfully.

On the American side the government has handled the negotiations, but most of the actual exchanges have been handled and financed through private channels, despite the absence of any counterpart private agencies in the Soviet Union. This remarkable demonstration of private initiative and freedom by American universities, foundations, professional societies and business groups has no doubt made a deep impression on many Soviet visitors and constitutes one of our unique advantages in the exchange.

The willingness of the Soviet Union to engage in such exchanges made it somewhat easier for other Eastern European countries to renew cultural contacts with the United States, though the experience thus far has varied widely—with Poland on the enthusiastic end of the scale and Rumania and Bulgaria on the other.

So far as labels were concerned, the official "educational and cultural exchange programs" of the federal government included only those administered by the State Department—the Fulbright and Smith-Mundt programs, cultural presentations, and Soviet exchange programs—but in fact many other federal agencies became increasingly involved in the field during the Fifties; under different program labels and with little reference to the State Department's exchange activities. The strong tendency was for each agency to go it alone.

The largest of these was the Defense Department's training programs in the United States for foreign military officers and men, which grew by 1960 to more than three times the number of foreign visitors handled annually under the Fulbright and Smith-Mundt programs. The next largest was the technical assistance program of the International Cooperation Administration which by 1960 was likewise bringing more foreigners to the United States and sending more Americans overseas in connection with training activities than the State Department's combined exchange programs.

Alarmed by the first Soviet "Sputnik," Congress enacted the National Defense Education Act to overcome various alleged weaknesses in American education. For the first time federal support was provided, among other things, to strengthen research and instruction in foreign areas and languages. This brought the United States Office of Education importantly into the field of international education, though mainly in terms of American students and scholars studying in our own institutions rather than overseas.

The American scientific community, encouraged and often financially supported by the federal government, also became increasingly involved in international affairs during the Fifties. By 1961 at least nine separate Federal "science" agencies were engaged in: (1) support for research in foreign countries, by either foreign or American scientists, (2) international educational and training programs which brought a few hundred foreigners to this country each year for scientific training and sent a somewhat smaller number of Americans abroad, and (3) the collection and dissemination of scientific information. Most of these activities directly affected educational institutions, here and abroad.

No one of these science programs alone is large, but collectively they make an impressive total, and the scale of effort has been rapidly expanding. Each agency has acted more or less independently, on its own statutory authority and budget and in keeping with what it regards as its own special mission. No one has been responsible for developing a comprehensive view of United States scientific requirements or potentialities for foreign assistance or for welding the activities of these various agencies into rational country plans overseas. Five of these agencies have established at least 14 science representatives or offices overseas, including three in Tokyo and two in London. It was estimated in 1960 that some 15,000 to 20,000 American scientists and engineers, often with support from one or another federal agency, were attending about 2,000 international meetings and conferences each year, sponsored by a vast array of international scientific organizations, private and governmental. There was no means for insuring appropriate United States representation at many such meetings or good quality United States participation in the secretariats of the more important organizations. The feeling of many observers was that the Soviet Union and Red China were taking these matters more seriously than the United States.

In short, scientific activity was expanding rapidly in the international arena; the United States had an enormous stake, but its activities were being managed in a most unscientific fashion. The biologists had a term for it—random proliferation. But this term fitted not only the science community; it characterized the total United States involvement in international educational and cultural affairs in the 1950's—federal and non-governmental alike—and it extended as well to the specialized agencies of the United Nations and to other international organizations.

Private efforts

Although it would be difficult to prove statistically, there seems little doubt that during the 1950's the private effort in this whole field—defined to include everything other than the federal government—grew in scope and magnitude even more than the federal effort and in the aggregate far exceeds the federal effort today, with the exception of technical assistance. To no small extent, however, the expanded private effort was stimulated by federal activities.

One important stimulus, for example, came from the fact that the Fulbright and Smith-Mundt exchange programs had been organized from the outset to involve extensive participation by university faculties, professional organizations and distinguished private citizens (especially through the Board of Foreign Scholarships, the United States Advisory Commission on Educational Exchange, and the United States National Commission for UNESCO) in the planning and actual conduct of the exchange programs. This close partnership not only helped mobilize private interest in this sphere of international affairs, but gave the government access to excellent outside talent and developed confidence at home and abroad in the objectivity, quality and nonpolitical character of the programs.

In developing the new international programs under the National Defense Education Act the Office of Education likewise turned extensively to universities, schools, and professional societies for help. The International Cooperation Administration increasingly enlisted American universities to carry out overseas projects on a contract basis, though a common complaint of the universities was that they were too often called in after the project was already designed. In any event, overseas experience on ICA contracts stimulated the interest of many faculty members in international affairs and has had a beneficial influence on the home campus. By the end of 1960, the ICA had contracts with over 50 universities involving overseas service activities in nearly as many countries.

Private foundations, particularly a few of the larger ones but some of the smaller ones as well, pioneered importantly in the international education field during the fifties, in a number of instances paving the way for larger government programs to follow. Private foundations—especially Rockefeller, Carnegie and Ford—took the lead, for example, in helping universities in this country to establish "area study centers" for such regions as South Asia, Eastern Europe, Africa, and Latin America. Later the National Defense Education Act, with careful attention to the pattern already set by private philanthropy, put federal funds in the same direction. Similarly, the private foundations paved the way for academic exchanges with Eastern European countries, and initiated important activities ahead of the government with respect to Africa.

Private philanthropic funds flowing into international affairs, largely into education and technical assistance, expanded enormously during the decade, both absolutely and as a proportion of total grants, though they still remained small relative to grants for domestic affairs. Curiously enough, despite the expanding international interests of American business, the corporation foundations did not display a similar interest in international affairs.

Literally hundreds of voluntary organizations across the country—national, state and local in scope—stepped up their activities in international affairs or entered the field for the first time. Some, such as the Institute of International Education and the National Association of Foreign Student Advisors, with heavy support from private foundations, had a specialized interest in this field. Many others, such as labor organizations, business groups, women's clubs and farm organizations had primary interests in other directions but nevertheless developed strong peripheral interests in international activities. President Eisenhower's call for a People to People program brought a strong response from a great variety of such organizations.

A survey in 1961 by the American Council of Voluntary Agencies for Foreign Services listed 98 different organizations—many of them church groups, foundations and specially organized agencies—significantly engaged in rendering overseas technical assistance and educational services.

These private activities reflected a greatly heightened concern with world affairs on the part of American people, a desire to strengthen our own international competence and position, to assist less fortunate peoples, and to forge stronger ties of friendship with other nations. But if the federal effort seemed fragmented, uncoordinated and at times confused, the private effort was vastly more so. Even in individual communities it was not unusual—and is still not today—to find an assortment of private organizations overlapping, competing and sometimes working at cross purposes to help foreign students, to send help abroad and to educate Americans about foreign affairs. The net effect undoubtedly, as with the federal effort, has been highly beneficial; but there is good reason to suppose that the total effort could be made considerably more effective with a modicum of cooperative planning.

International Organizations

As the largest contributor to a host of international agencies, the United States also expanded its effort in the international educational, scientific and cultural field through these multilateral channels.

Virtually every United Nations specialized agency—UNESCO, ILO, WHO, the Special Fund, FAO and others—expanded its educational activities during the Fifties, though UNESCO was the primary agent. The over-all results still await careful evaluation, but meantime it is clear that in matters of joint planning and unification of effort international agencies are not unlike federal and private agencies. Harlan Cleveland observed shortly before becoming Assistant Secretary of State for International Organizational Affairs in 1961 that the "deficiencies of the international machinery now in existence are quite obvious. The UN specialized agencies are too sovereign, too much inclined toward functional particularism, and too little coordinated in rational 'country programs.' "

Cleveland's comment was not intended, however, to disparage the importance of multilateral agencies. On the contrary, he observed that, "After more than a decade of experience with foreign aid, it is clear that bilateral relationships have serious limitations, especially when they touch on central issues of economic and social policy. . . ." He saw great advantage in working through private channels where feasible, citing the effective work of the Ford Foundation overseas, but when it comes to "the wide range of activities which can only be carried on at the government level," he observed, "there is a strong case for making effective multilateral organization our primary agent for economic development and doing our best to persuade all other industrial countries to use the same agency for promoting sound progress in emergent countries."

Despite the much criticized scatteration of programs by UNESCO and the lack of a sufficiently unified effort by the UN specialized agencies, there can be little doubt that much good has been accomplished through these channels, not only toward helping the developing countries but toward strengthening peaceful educational, scientific, and cultural interchange among the advanced nations. UNESCO has clearly earned the confidence of the emergent nations of Asia, Africa, and Latin America, even if it has fallen far short of providing all the help they want and if some of its specific projects and activities have been of doubtful value. This confidence is an enormously important asset to build on in the future.

To a lesser degree various regional organizations with which the United States is associated, particularly the Organization of American States and the Organization for Economic Cooperation and Development (formerly OEEC), have also shown an expanding interest in educational, scientific, and cultural affairs. They too represent an important potential though their accomplishments thus far have been modest. It was unfortunate that OAS lacked the organizational strength in these fields to take strong initiatives at the outset of the Alliance for Progress.

The United States was not without some responsibility for the fragmentation of international organization programs in this field during the Fifties and for some of the notable shortcomings. After enthusiastic support for UNESCO at the outset, the United States interest dwindled, the efforts to recruit good quality Americans for UNESCO work were at best spasmodic, the formulation of United States positions on UNESCO matters was largely relegated to people far down in the bureaucratic hierarchy, and in the face of cold war pressures the American preference for bilateral action grew steadily stronger.

The legacy of a decade of expansion

The Fifties, in short, were a period of unplanned proliferation of international educational and cultural activities on all sides, and while this constituted progress it also created a heritage of problems which the Kennedy Administration had to face in early 1961.

Not least of the problems was that the Fulbright and Smith-Mundt programs, the core of the official exchange programs, after a strong start in the late Forties suddenly slowed down and even lost ground in the

Fifties. The State Department's exchange budget (excluding the new "cultural presentations program") was actually lower in 1957 than in 1951, and the number of exchangees fell in this period from 7,263 to 6,329. Slow recovery set in after 1957 but did not catch up with expanding requirements. Over-all from 1951 to 1961 the number of foreign countries involved in these exchanges doubled, but the total number of exchangees rose by less than one quarter.

One obvious reason for this slow-down was that educational and cultural affairs had not yet come to be regarded by top officials as having a vital bearing on our foreign relations. They were "good things to do" but not in the same class as political, economic, and military affairs which dealt with the "practical realities" and the "serious business" of foreign policy. The exchange program was an orphan in the State Department. It was not, for example, a promising place for an able and ambitious young foreign service officer to "get ahead"; over 15 years not one who did a tour of duty there rose later to the rank of Ambassador. It is not surprising, therefore, that Congressional appropriations committees also lacked enthusiasm for these programs, and that this particular item became the annual area of compromise in the Department's over-all request for appropriations.

There was also a corresponding tendency toward indifference on the part of the government concerning the educational and cultural activities of international organizations. Responsibility for working with them in educational, scientific and cultural matters, for developing strong policy positions, and for exerting strong leadership in their councils, was scattered among the federal agencies and even within the State Department. There were no clear guidelines for relating our bilateral efforts to the multilateral efforts of international organizations, though obviously both were important. As a result, we tended to dwell upon the former and neglect the latter, thereby weakening our role of leadership in international organizations.

The private sector had demonstrated a great willingness and capacity to help, but stronger federal leadership and guidance were needed to stimulate a still larger and better directed private involvement. There was need here as in the federal government and international organizations for a more unified effort.

ATTEMPTS TO UNIFY THE NATIONAL EFFORT

The accomplishments and shortcomings in this new sector of American foreign policy were no secret; they had been subjected to close scrutiny by several expert studies in the late Fifties. Under Congressional prodding, the State Department had requested President J. L. Morrill of the University of Minnesota to examine the situation, and his 1956 report strongly recommended the creation of an Assistant Secretary of State to be Coordinator for Cultural and Technical Exchange with clear authority to harmonize the exchange programs of State and the International Cooperation Administration and the relationship of both with the academic community and other nongovernment groups. He also urged larger funds for the State Department's declining exchange programs. Later the Legislative Reference Service, at the request of Congress, prepared a comprehensive survey of Government Programs in International Education (published in early 1959) which revealed for the first time the enormous diversity and fragmentation of federal activities in this field.

Secretary Christian Herter was the first to initiate practical efforts to strengthen the organization and prestige of these activities within the Department, but he was unsuccessful in securing a White House mandate to insure inter-agency coordination. His new Special Assistant for Educational and Cultural Affairs, Robert Thayer, initiated useful efforts to strengthen government relations with the private sector and endeavored to bring about some coordination of federal activities, but in his ambiguous role of Special Assistant and lacking a clearcut "driver's license" to negotiate the cobbled roads of the federal bureaucracy, he was extremely handicapped.

Partly by happy circumstance, the strengths and weaknesses of the national effort by 1960 were brought into sharp focus, along with many useful guidelines for the future, by a spate of expert reports which appeared within a few weeks of President John F. Kennedy's inauguration, most of them initiated before the election by the previous administration or by private organizations. They included:

The University and World Affairs, A report by a distinguished committee sponsored by the Ford Foundation, J. L. Morrill, Chairman; John B. Howard, Study Director. (Available from Ford Foundation.)

Toward a National Effort in International Educational and Cultural Affairs, A report prepared for the United States Advisory Commission of Educational Exchange, Department of State, Dr. Walter H. C. Laves (Available from Superintendent of Documents, U.S. Government Printing Office).

Report of the President's Committee on Information Activities Abroad, appointed by President Eisenhower; Mansfield Sprague, Chairman; Waldemar A. Neilsen, Executive Director (summarized in Bulletin, Department of State, Feb. 6, 1961 issue).

The College and University in International Affairs, 1959-60 Annual Report of the Carnegie Foundation for the Advancement of teaching (New York).

Report on Exchange of Persons, by an *ad hoc* task force appointed by President-elect Kennedy; Chairman James M. Davis.

A Report to the President of the United States, transmitted by Kenneth Holland, President of the Institute for International Education.

In late 1960, the Senate Foreign Relations Committee, under the leadership of Senator Fulbright, had also assembled a large body of expert opinion with a view to consolidating and strengthening federal legislation in this field (which resulted in the Fulbright-Hays Act of 1961).

There was striking agreement among these various experts that the national effort in this field was too small, too scattered and uncoordinated, too unrelated to specific important objectives, and enjoyed too little top level support.

The 1959 survey for Congress had found some two dozen Federal agencies active in international education, but it found no one in charge. "It seems clear," the report said, "that there is not only the lack of over-all policy and the lack of an over-all coordinating agency but even the lack of comprehensive, organized information on what all the agencies of the government have been doing in this field."

Dr. Laves placed much of the responsibility squarely upon those charged with the conduct of the nation's foreign policy: ". . . our educational and cultural activities enjoy a low priority in the administration of our foreign relations."

Taken together, these various reports made clear to the new Kennedy Administration the need for a stronger, more unified, more efficient and effective national effort. This would require stronger federal leadership and central policy guidance; more joint planning and coordination of effort among all agencies—at home and overseas; more cooperation among private agencies, and between them and the federal government; a general strengthening of all organizations and personnel concerned; fresh program ideas; a consolidation of legislation; more attention to UNESCO and other international organizations, and most important, a higher national priority and larger financial support for the whole effort.

EARLY ACTIONS BY THE KENNEDY ADMINISTRATION

The new President acted promptly on one key recommendation by creating an Assistant Secretary of State for Educational and Cultural Affairs. In a press statement on February 27, 1961, he said, ". . . this whole field is urgently in need of imaginative policy development, unification and vigorous direction." He would look to the Secretary of State, aided by the new Assistant Secretary, "to exercise primary responsibility for policy guidance and program direction of governmental activities in this field."

Acknowledging the crucial importance of educational and cultural affairs to United States foreign policy, the President observed that there was no better way to help the new nations of Latin America, Africa and

Asia, "than by assisting them to develop their human resources through education. . . . Likewise, there is no better way to strengthen our bonds of understanding and friendship with older nations than through educational and cultural interchange."

President Kennedy then appealed to the educational community, private foundations and voluntary organizations for a still greater effort, noting that "These institutions represent our national resource base for helping new countries educationally and strengthening our cultural ties with old ones."

Private organizations and the academic community quickly responded to this fresh assertion of federal leadership, with new ideas for program improvement, a new willingness to cooperate, and a new burst of private effort. Representatives of many foreign governments and officials of international organizations also made it clear that they welcomed this new American initiative.

Congress contributed to the effort by enacting the Fulbright-Hays Act in the fall of 1961, by an overwhelming majority. The new law consolidated the old Fulbright and Smith-Mundt laws and various other scattered legislative provisions, removed a variety of major and minor obstacles to effective administration, and added several useful new authorities. Cosponsor Wayne Hays of Ohio later told the newly appointed United States Advisory Commission on International Educational and Cultural Affairs, headed by Dr. John W. Gardner, "This law is intended to give all the possible authority needed to develop this field adequately. If you don't find what you need, ask your lawyers to look harder."

In the year that followed, a wide variety of actions was initiated by the new Administration toward unifying and strengthening the national effort, and extensive plans were prepared for future improvement.

The following specific issues received particular attention from the new Assistant Secretary's office, working in close cooperation with other federal agencies and numerous private experts and organizations: (1) better planning and great emphasis in the AID program on human resources development in Africa, Latin America and Asia as the *sine qua non* for economic and social development; (2) new educational techniques, curriculum reform and more books for these areas; (3) improving the experiences of foreign students, and especially African students in the United States; (4) strengthening American education in world affairs, including the study of foreign languages, areas and relations; (5) teaching English overseas as a second language; (6) improving overseas schools for American dependents and strengthening American-sponsored colleges in the Middle East; (7) encouraging the exchange of educational and cultural TV programs and films, (8) broadening and improving the "cultural presentations" program, with more accent on young talent, and preparing to initiate a "reverse flow" of foreign artistic presentations to the United States; (9) strengthening cultural relations with specific countries such as Japan, the United Arab Republic, Spain, Poland, and the Soviet Union; (10) strengthening United States cooperation with and participation in UNESCO; (11) nourishing the cultural vitality of West Berlin; (12) preparing to follow through on the new Fulbright-Hays Act; (13) fostering "country planning" by United States missions abroad; (14) strengthening federal cooperation with private agencies; (15) encouraging better coordination of international organizations; (16) providing a strong role for education in the Alliance for Progress; and (17) reorganizing and strengthening the State Department's Bureau of Educational and Cultural Affairs to provide more effective focus on specific geographic areas.

Attention was also concentrated upon clarifying and articulating the basic philosophy, concepts, and program and policy guidelines that should govern the national effort. These are dealt with in the following section of this chapter.

In summary, the first year and one half of the new Kennedy Administration saw a considerable strengthening of the national effort in this vital sector of the nation's foreign policy and foreign relations, based on extensive cooperation of many persons and agencies both in and outside the federal government. Many top officers in the foreign service attached new importance to these activities as an element of foreign policy; many actions were initiated in both the public and private sector to improve the quality, size and effectiveness of existing programs; and to achieve a more unified national effort; and many plans were devised for further improvement.

A new phase of our national effort in this field was begun, but there were no miracles and a very great deal remained to be accomplished. Within the federal government there were still many inherited deficiencies of organization and personnel to be overcome, along with old bureaucratic habits, inertias, and vested interests. And not least important was the problem of persuading the reluctant House Appropriations Committee that these activities were as vital to the success of the nation's foreign policy goals as economic aid and military expenditures, though requiring far less money.

The full success of the Administration's fresh efforts in this field would require time, sustained effort, and strong day-to-day support from top State Department, White House and other Administration officials who inevitably were preoccupied with current crises, negotiations and other pressing matters. It would require also strong and sustained support from busy Congressional, educational and civic leaders.

GUIDELINES FOR FUTURE ACTION

As we face the future, perhaps our greatest asset is the rapidly emerging new national consensus on where we should go from here. This consensus rests on the conviction that educational and cultural affairs are as important as political, military and economic affairs to achieving the long range goals of American foreign policy and the United Nations Charter. It holds that educational and cultural programs are as practical in purpose as they are lofty; that they belong not on the periphery of our foreign relations but in the mainstream. They are no mere "fringe benefits" but contribute importantly to the serious business of foreign relations by complementing and reinforcing all our other international activities—our political diplomacy, our economic and military programs. They add to all these a much needed flexibility, versatility and depth. Every important objective in the spectrum of our foreign policy goals— short run or long run—can be importantly served by them, and sometimes by no other means. They are not a panacea, nor by themselves sufficient, but they are a vital and indispensable component of a well-balanced foreign policy.

This consensus further holds that, for their greatest effectiveness, these educational and cultural activities must be planned and conducted in close conjunction with all other international programs, both at home and overseas; they should be an integral part of each "country plan." This imperative for maximum effectiveness applies equally to governmental and private efforts, and requires maximum cooperation between the two. For their greatest effectiveness educational and cultural activities must also be directed consciously at specific objectives, country by country and within the United States, not treated as ends in themselves.

Among the paramount objectives to be served are these:

First, to strengthen American education and our national competence in world affairs.

Second, to develop an accurate knowledge and understanding of the United States by foreigners, especially those who shape the youth and policies and destinies of their own nation.

Third, to strengthen the Atlantic Community and our partnership with Japan which constitute the core of the free world's strength and greatest promise.

Fourth, to help emerging nations build strong, viable and independent societies whose values and goals are compatible with our own, though their economic and other institutions and customs may differ.

Fifth, to reduce dangerous tensions and broaden the channels of constructive communication, understanding and agreement with communist nations.

Sixth, to advance human knowledge and human welfare generally, and to strengthen the mechanisms for international cooperation.

To advance these broader objectives, if we interpret the new consensus correctly, the following specific policies should be pursued:

Give as much weight to improving the *quality* of programs as to expanding their size.

Give much heavier emphasis, greater visability and more systematic treatment in our foreign aid programs to the development of education and human resources in emerging nations.

Clarify for each important task the best division of labor between governmental and private effort, and encourage greater private initiative in those matters which can best be done privately.

Give greater responsibility, latitude, and support to academic institutions and private agencies entrusted with the conduct of federal programs.

Seek greater collaboration with Western European nations and Japan in planning, financing and conducting programs, both among ourselves and in relation to less developed countries.

Increase our efforts to work through international and regional organizations, and particularly strengthen United States leadership in UNESCO.

Balance our efforts aimed primarily at short-run results with a heavy and steady emphasis on programs that will produce long-run, lasting benefits.

Raise educational and cultural affairs from the subordinate status they have had relative to information activities and the physical aspects of economic development in our overseas missions, and give greater prestige to them in the career services of the Department of State, USIA and AID.

Give more emphasis in exchange programs to inviting foreign visitors who have been strong critics of the United States, and liberalize visa regulations to make this possible.

Put more accent on youth in exchange programs, on labor, women and intellectual leaders, and on all the influential progressive elements of less developed countries.

In the training of foreign military personnel, give attention not only to the arts of warfare but to the arts of peaceful, democratic government.

In all programs, give emphasis to building institutional strengths, in both the United States and other countries, and particularly those institutions which are vital for a viable democracy.

Increase our educational and cultural interchange with communist nations as rapidly as feasible even while political tensions prevail, taking care to safeguard our own vital interests but avoiding unproductive rigidity and quibbling in small matters.

Most Americans who have given careful thought to the great issues of world peace and to the potential contribution of educational and cultural affairs would, we believe, subscribe in general to the foregoing framework for a national policy to guide both governmental and private endeavors, though many would no doubt phrase things differently and most would have other points to add. It would be a long step forward, however, if the educational, civic, governmental and other leaders of our nation could agree that in fact we agree on this much.

A PROGRAM FOR ACTION

Within this framework there are abundant opportunities to strengthen present public and private programs, quickly and substantially. The few discussed below merit early action.

More emphasis on educational development overseas

A serious defect of our past foreign aid programs has been the haphazard approach and inadequate attention to the development of human resources, which frustrates the whole purpose of foreign aid.

"For many countries seeking development," Professor Max Millikan of M.I.T. observed recently, "the key factor inhibiting economic growth is the absence of an effective educational system in the broadest sense of that term. No matter what the availability of physical resources or financing, neither economic nor political development is possible without an educational system which is efficient. . . ."

The new aid program of the Kennedy Administration gives greater recognition to this matter, but the good intentions still need to be expressed more fully in action. One obstacle is the shortage of what Professor Fred Harbison of Princeton has called "educational strategists" who combine the virtues of a good educational generalist with an understanding of the processes of economic, social and political development and a sensitivity to cultural differences. They are needed not only by the Agency for International Development but by international organizations such as UNESCO and the World Bank and by developing countries themselves, to help design educational development plans and priorities that fit each country's needs and its over-all economic and social development plans.

Thus far, there is no recruiting and training program in the United States to produce such persons. During 1961 and 1962, the new Agency for International Development made disappointing progress in finding the type and quality of personnel needed for the vigorous emphasis on development of human resources which both the President and Congress have called for.

With the tide running strongly toward putting the bulk of United States aid in loans rather than grants and technical assistance, and given the inclination of loan officers to view physical property as a better investment than people, educational development faces an uphill struggle.

Until everyone up and down the line becomes convinced that developing human abilities is as important as building roads, steel mills and fertilizer factories, and that the two must be kept reasonably balanced, our aid program will fall far short of its potential, and the laudable goals of social and economic development will be frustrated.

On the encouraging side is the growing recognition that developing countries cannot meet their pressing educational needs simply by spending more money to expand their existing educational system, which is typically a copy of some industrialized nation's system. There must be a revolution of curriculum, methods and virtually every other aspect of education if these countries are to build educational systems which fit their needs and their pocketbooks. The United States is uniquely in a position to assist in this matter after a decade of unprecedented innovation, experimentation and radical change in our own educational system. But the steps thus far in this direction have been very limited.

Better quality programs for foreign students

The central issue here is not whether there are too few or too many foreign students. Less than 10 per cent come here under government-sponsored programs; the rest come as a consequence of private initiatives and decisions, and the prospects are for a continuing increase in their number. The central issue right now is how to improve the personal and academic experience of all foreign students who come here, regardless of how they came or how many there are.

To meet this need, the State Department in 1961 proposed a Ten-Point Program of public and private actions which has been enthusiastically received and given substantial private support already. A further increase in private effort and federal financial support is required.

This program calls for: (1) acceptance of a continuing obligation by all sponsors of foreign students; (2) strengthening overseas facilities for counselling, selection and placement; (3) improved orientation and English language practice; (4) better academic programs for foreign students; (5) improved advisory services in colleges and universities; (6) better co-ordination of private organizations and improvement of community programs; (7) broader opportunities for effective summer work experiences;

(8) sustained relations with foreign alumni after they return home; (9) more effective utilization of returned foreign students by their own countries; and (10) more research and evaluation.

Improvement of foreign leaders and specialists programs

Several thousand foreign leaders come here each year as guests of our government—including foreign government officials (from promising young people of lower rank to cabinet ministers), legislators, leading journalists and broadcasters, civic leaders, lawyers, outstanding women and labor leaders, top educators, and a variety of specialists. Such visits have been highly valuable but could be substantially improved at modest cost by: (1) reducing red-tape and giving our embassies more latitude; (2) increasing the number and the services of reception centers in this country; (3) improving the program arrangements for visitors; (4) consolidating the AID and State Department leader programs, at least in the United States; (5) improving escort and interpreter services; (6) improving hospitality and entertainment; (7) making greater use of specialized national and local professional civic organizations.

More attention than in the past should be given to developing closer relations between youth leaders, labor, intellectual and women leaders in other countries and our own, since in all our nations these groups can be important positive forces for democratic progress. Likewise, the leader and specialist exchange programs should forge stronger links among the creative writers, artists, composers and other cultural leaders and innovators across national lines.

Improvement of American professors and specialists programs

These should be programs of the highest distinction, sending abroad our most eminent professors, writers, composers, scientists and talented people in all major fields and in adequate numbers. To accomplish this, more help will be needed from professional societies, foundation officers and others familiar with the nation's accomplished leaders and promising younger people in each major field, to help identify and recruit the best people to serve overseas. More flexibility is required in existing State Department exchange programs to accommodate the circumstances of individual professors so that they can go abroad for less than a full academic year (as now required) if necessary, or stay for more than one academic year if feasible. The financial arrangements must be improved to enable a distinguished scholar to serve abroad under the State Department's program without heavy out-of-pocket costs to himself (which is now the case). The annual prohibition in appropriations legislation against payment of travel costs for the wife of a professor going abroad for a substantial period should be eliminated. The same general principles apply to the "American Specialist" program which should be made entirely invitational and conducted with quality standards of excellence.

Strengthening United States education

More attention should be given to strengthening American educational institutions through existing international programs, by better planning and integration of effort on the part of public and private agencies alike.

The priority goals should be: (1) to overhaul school and college curriculums to reflect the realities of a changing world; (2) to develop cooperative groups of neighboring small colleges to share scarce and costly resources required to strengthen their world affairs studies, and to pool their strengths for joint research and overseas projects; (3) to strengthen advanced training and research in foreign areas and languages and in fields of international specialization where competent manpower is needed by the nation; (4) to improve and expand foreign language instruction in the schools and colleges; (5) to train and retrain teachers in all aspects of world affairs at all levels of education; (6) to improve opportunities for students, teachers, and scholars to study abroad; and (7) to enlarge the academic manpower pool so that academic institutions can render important services overseas without prejudice to their own students.

Strengthening government personnel

There is great need to upgrade the quality, competence and status of our educational and cultural representatives and advisors overseas, in our embassies, aid missions and USIS offices. We already have a number of excellent people, despite adverse conditions, but in far too many cases we are inadequately represented. This is not the fault of the individuals involved but of the whole system of recruitment, selection, training, status, promotion incentives, in-service improvement opportunities, and general working conditions. Far-reaching improvements are needed because the ultimate effectiveness of our national effort depends heavily upon the calibre of our overseas representatives.

Civilian agencies should catch up with the military services in providing advanced training opportunities for promising employees. All agencies sending personnel overseas could learn much from the Peace Corps training program. To save here is false economy.

If cultural officers on home duty, for example, could spend some time teaching and studying at a university, they would enrich the university and return overseas better equipped to perform their duties. As interpreters of American education and culture abroad, they need to participate in it at home from time to time. This is not accomplished by a temporary desk job in Washington.

Books, films and television

Despite newer media, the book has lost none of its importance as an efficient "learning machine" for communicating knowledge, concepts, values and culture.

There is a "book gap" in Latin America, Africa and Asia today greater than in Abraham Lincoln's America, and the communists are working harder than the free world nations to fill it.

The USIA book program has been excellent, but much too small and too narrow in variety to meet the needs of developing countries. The communists are said to have spent more on books in 1960 in one Latin American country than USIA spent in the whole world. Relatively trivial AID program funds have gone into books—largely technical books relating to specific training projects. Here again, the AID programs need a fresh, broader, and more realistic concept of what is required for successful economic and social development.

There is need for a massive attack on this book problem, aimed at (a) making available a large supply and wide variety of the best American and other free world books—textbooks, technical and reference books, good literature, and all types of books having a high educational and cultural quality, (b) developing indigenous publishing and distribution facilities in less developed countries; (c) helping them create their own textbooks and literature, and (d) making available in American and European markets the best writings of the developing countries.

Our private publishers and university presses have much to contribute to such an effort, along with the government. It cannot fail to be a highly productive investment for this nation and others, and increasingly it will become self-financing. In some countries it would undoubtedly pay to use available funds for fewer United States technical experts and more books.

Throughout the world vast numbers of people are learning about the United States—or think they are—from our commercial films and television shows. A small proportion of these are excellent examples of our finest achievements in the visual arts, music, drama and documentaries. Many others are certainly not "bad"—they are entertaining and reflect something of our humor, folklore, strengths and weaknesses, our progress and our unresolved problems. A disturbingly high proportion, however, are just plain horrible and create a seriously distorted picture of American life. What is intended as simple entertainment for American audiences is often educational for a foreign audience, or mis-educational.

Taken as a whole, it seems fair to say that American commercial films and television programs, while there is much good in them, present a lopsided and in many ways harmful picture of American society to the rest of the world. No amount of denials by industry leaders in after-dinner speeches at home can conceal this hard fact from observant Americans who travel in Latin America, Asia, and Africa. It is no excuse to say that "we are giving them what they want." They will take anything they can get, and we are teaching them to want our worst, not our best.

The remedy is not government censorship, but an abundance of good judgment, self-restraint and patriotic concern by exporters. What is most needed is to balance the diet of lighter entertainment with a large infusion of first quality educational, cultural and documentary programs that display the more serious, creative, and cultivated side of American life. Commercial producers and especially our educational television system can be very helpful here.

English as a second language

The explosive demand to learn English—from Tokyo to Djakarta and from Leopoldville to Lima—has outstripped the ability of English-speaking countries to meet it, yet it is vitally important to do so. It is a major means by which others can come to know the English-speaking world, to know its values and aspirations, to tap its intellectual, technical and cultural resources.

The bottleneck is the limited supply of specialized manpower to teach English. The solution, obviously, is to find ways to teach English well with a much lower "input" of this specialized manpower per pupil and a greater emphasis on effective means of self-instruction. The search is on for such means, but the effort needs to be greatly intensified, in concert with other English-speaking countries. A far-reaching technological breakthrough here will also help meet our own foreign language needs. Meantime we must also train more teachers in this field.

Cultural presentations—a two-way flow

The cultural presentations program of the Department of State, earlier described, is no larger now than when it began several years ago. To meet worldwide needs we spend $2.5 million each year—about equal to the production budget of one Grade A movie in Hollywood. Meanwhile many new countries have emerged, and a major cultural exchange with the Soviet Union has been undertaken, all on the same sized budget. The communist countries have stepped up sharply their competing cultural programs, which are much larger than ours.

A reorientation and large expansion of the program is needed, along with strengthening its administration. More small American groups should visit small and medium communities where American perform-ances are unknown. Much greater use should be made of young artistic talent from our colleges and universities, especially to establish rapport with youthful audiences in Latin America and elsewhere. We are pres-ently only scratching the surface of this program's potential, not for lack of talent and cooperation but for lack of funds and limited administrative capabilities.

The new Fulbright-Hays Act authorizes encouragement of a reverse flow of foreign artistic groups to the United States for non-commercial performances. This will enrich our own culture and provide new insights into others. Not least important, it will demonstrate our interest and re-spect for the cultural attainments of others and provide those nations to whom we have given economic help a dignified opportunity to send us something in return. It will take time and great care to develop this reverse flow for it involves many sticky problems, but a start should be made forthwith. Academic institutions and professional organizations are best equipped to manage such activities.

Training soldiers for peaceful progress

In a recent year the Defense Department trained some 28,000 foreign officers and men in the United States—as noted earlier, more than three times the total of foreign visitors brought here under the Fulbright and Smith-Mundt programs. The training was almost exclusively technical, at military installations.

We know from experience that many of these foreign military men will play extremely important roles in their own turbulent societies that extend far beyond military affairs. Waldemar Nielsen, Executive Director of the President's Committee on Information Activities Abroad (the Sprague Committee), pointed out in the *New York Times Magazine* in June 1961, "Most of the military leaders who have seized power or at-tempted to seize power in recent years in Turkey, Pakistan, Korea and France are ex-participants in the United States military training pro-grams. Moreover, in many areas of the world where political conditions are chaotic, military leaders are playing an increasingly decisive role."

A classic example was the military takeover in Peru in July 1962 by officers trained by the United States, using an American tank to break into the grounds of a democratically elected President.

We should provide opportunities for at least some of these military trainees to get a broader experience. Some, for example, might go to university campuses for a few weeks to take special courses in public administration, history and other social sciences. This would show them a different side of American life and help equip them to strengthen the institutions of democracy in their own country. It would be naïve to assume that a short course in democracy would suddenly reverse long-standing traditions of military dominance in many of these countries, but to turn our backs on the problem and proceed simply to strengthen the military can be a fatal policy.

Our military services have followed the enlightened policy of enabling our own promising officers to learn more about economic, social and political affairs at civilian universities, at the National War College and elsewhere. Among other things this has helped reinforce our tradition of civilian control of government, the economy and the military itself. We should do no less for visiting foreign military officers who often are in even greater need of such experience.

THE MAGNITUDE OF AN ADEQUATE EFFORT

It is impossible to speak in precise terms about the magnitude of effort required when there does not yet exist: (1) a clear and comprehensive picture of the present national effort and its costs; (2) a quantitative assessment of the needs of American education and for specialized American manpower in the field of world affairs; (3) a country-by-country analysis of needs and opportunities, and priorities, for United States educational and cultural programs; and (4) an appraisal of the availability of institutional and manpower resources required to mount a substantially enlarged effort.

It should also be remembered that the rate at which expenditures—public and private—can be effectively increased is governed by the rate at which competent administrative capabilities can be enlarged.

Despite all these limitations, however, it is clear that a substantial increase in effort in the immediate future is both urgently needed and feasible. As a general order of magnitude we should think in terms not of a 10 or 20 per cent increase per year but of a doubling or trebling of our effort over the next three to five years, with appropriate variations by geographic areas and by types of programs. These programs have lagged too long and there is a large accumulated gap that needs urgently to be closed.

The point may be illustrated by two of the federal budgets involved. The gross outlays of the State Department's Bureau of Educational and Cultural Affairs in fiscal year 1962, including a substantial proportion in foreign currencies, was under $50 million—to cover all types of exchanges of persons, cultural presentations, support for American studies and American-sponsored schools overseas, and a variety of special projects. If proper personnel and other administrative support were provided, it would be feasible and highly desirable to expand under the new Fulbright-Hays Act to a level of $100 million by fiscal year 1964 and $200 million in another two to three years. Major emphasis should be given to strengthening programs with respect to Latin America and Africa.

The operating budget of USIA in fiscal year 1962 was just over $100 million. A large proportion went to current informational activities—the fast news media and the Voice of America—as distinct from books, libraries, work with universities and other longer term educational and cultural efforts. Budget stringencies have lately forced a sharp reduction of these latter efforts in Western Europe—such as the closing down of United States libraries and cultural centers—at the very time the President has been urging a strengthening of the Atlantic Community. By tradition, and from the heritage of the psychological warfare approach of the Second World War, the USIA gives priority to its current news efforts, but the time has come to give greater support to its longer term educational and cultural efforts. This will require a sizeable increase in USIA's budget for such purposes. Even looked at from a short term cold war and propaganda point of view, it is here much more than in the fast media that the Sino-Soviet Bloc countries are running circles around the United States in the level of their effort.

The Sprague Committee estimated in 1960, perhaps generously, that total government expenditures on the whole spectrum of informational, educational and cultural programs, broadly defined, "constitutes roughly one per cent of the approximate total of $50 billion spent annually for national security." This does seem a bit unbalanced.

The comparative ease—and at times eagerness—with which money is appropriated for military purposes is in dramatic contrast to the difficulties of securing adequate appropriations for educational and cultural programs. It will take special effort by the President, the Secretary of State and others to persuade Congress that the relatively modest financial requirements for an adequate effort in the educational and cultural sector of foreign policy are extremely vital to the nation's international goals. This effort has yet to be made.

Along with increased federal funds, there is equal need for more funds from other sources. Local school systems, private and tax-supported colleges and universities, all require additional funds to improve themselves in world affairs and to play a larger role in this total national effort. Nonprofit national organizations that play key roles in mobilizing the private sector and linking it with government, or that render critically important operating services with respect to foreign students, foreign educational development and the like, require considerable strengthening. Much is expected of these organizations. They are called upon constantly for help but too seldom are given help in return. Typically they are forced to conduct their operations on a financial shoestring, but then are criticized for not doing a quality job, or for letting certain problems or opportunities go unattended. They have a crucial role to play in our pluralistic society, but they need adequate financing to play it well, and the financing must come largely from private sources if they are to preserve their essential private character.

It was encouraging, in this light, to see substantial long-range general support recently extended by two major foundations to the American Council on Education which is strengthening its activities in world affairs. Similar basic support in adequate amounts from a wide variety of sources—a few large foundations cannot and should not carry the load alone—is needed by such other organizations as the Institute for International Education, the African-American Institute, the National Association of Foreign Student Advisors, the People to People complex and the major national educational organizations and professional societies.

At the community level, there is also need for more private support to those organizations that have demonstrated their dedication and competence to do useful work in one or another aspect of world affairs.

With all these needs, individual and corporate donors as well as foundations should have no difficulty finding practical ways to contribute to the strengthening of American foreign relations and to a better world through educational and cultural means.

THE STRATEGY OF ACTION

It is clear, as we said at the outset, that the main problem of the future is not where to go but how to get there. There is no shortage of good ideas on policies, programs, priorities and organizational improvements; the central need is to translate them into action. This calls for a strategy of action.

Conviction and support

The foremost requirement of this strategy is not better organization but stronger conviction and stronger support—on the part of top Administration and Congressional leaders and top civic and educational leaders, whose views and actions are crucial to shaping the nation's priorities and the direction of its effort.

These educational and cultural activities have suffered long from good words unmatched by practical deeds, particularly when it comes to money or to overcoming bureaucratic impediments.

The scattered voices of those inside and outside government who see most clearly the urgent need for a greater national effort have never been marshalled—as they have been on many other issues—in a loud chorus demanding action. There is need for leadership to explain the importance and to rally the forces of support.

Outside the government this leadership belongs especially with major educational organizations, working closely with all other interested parties. Inside government it belongs with the Secretary of State, along with the President. The heads of such agencies as USIA, AID, and HEW are required to lend their active and sustained support.

All these leaders are unmercifully pressured by many other demands and must divide their energies by some scale of priorities. Until they give this underdeveloped area of our foreign policy a greater claim on their attention, however, it is hard to see how the national effort will rise to the need.

Organization and leadership

A second requirement of strategy is improvement of organization and administration. By their nature these activities will inevitably be widely scattered among many private and public agencies. This scatteration, if held within reason, has the virtue of tapping many sources of specialized strength. Given this inevitable scatteration, there is imperative need for strong leadership and central policy guidance, efficient exchange of information, cooperative planning, and in some cases, joint operations, among all the agencies involved. This applies to private as well as federal agencies. As the report, *The University & World Affairs* points out, there is need for much more systematic cooperation among academic institutions and various private organizations active in this field. And there is need for fuller interchange and cooperation between government and the private sector.

The day-to-day leadership, policy guidance and concerted promotion of better harmonized efforts, both public and private, must come, if it is to come at all, from the Assistant Secretary of State for Educational and Cultural Affairs, with the sturdy support of the Secretary and President. He must free himself sufficiently from the operational demands of the Department's Bureau of Educational and Cultural Affairs to play this broader role of leadership. He must have a clear mandate and sufficient staff to help him, which he does not now have, and he must have ample support from above. The time may soon come when effective leadership by the Department of State in this field will require, as some have already recommended, an Under Secretary for Educational, Scientific and Cultural Affairs on a parity with similar present positions for economic and political affairs.

Outside the government there is no single locus of leadership toward a unified effort. The heads of all major educational and professional organizations, voluntary groups and foundations must share the responsibility, but they will exercise it best if they work closely and frequently together.

The new organization, Education in World Affairs, financed by the

Ford Foundation and Carnegie Corporation, holds promise of making a major contribution toward greater cohesion in the private sector and more productive relations with government.

The question is often asked whether the situation would not be greatly improved in the federal government by some scheme of drastic reorganization and consolidation—such as putting the State Department's Bureau of Educational and Cultural Affairs into USIA, or USIA's educational and cultural activities into the Bureau, or consolidating AID educational activities with those of the State Department, or creating a new operating agency to bring all these international educational, scientific and cultural activities together under one roof, free of the crusty constraints of the older organization. A good case can no doubt be made, at least on paper, for one or another such reorganization, but as a practical matter right now it might well have the negative effect of creating confusion and dissension which would slow down the whole effort for a considerable time.

There is also a widely held view that government-sponsored educational and cultural exchanges and related programs should not be handled overseas by the USIS as they now are because this, in the eyes of many foreigners, American educators and others, associates them too closely with propaganda. While this point is often greatly exaggerated and tends to become more a fetish than a well-grounded fact, it certainly has some merit. But here again, given the present long standing arrangements, there are no neat and easy alternatives. Moreover, the arguments are not all on one side.

This is not to say, however, that the present pattern of governmental organization, especially with regard to State, USIA, and AID, is satisfactory or could not be improved by major surgery. After all, it is more the result of historical accident than thoughtful design, and even if it once was satisfactory—which is doubtful—times have changed.

We do not have a tidy reorganization plant to present here, but we do believe that deep consideration should be given to developing one which might be put into effect in stages. We would also emphasize, however, that no reorganization plan is going to produce miracles, or even substantial improvements, unless accompanied by other measures to give stronger leadership, higher priority, better staffing, and better budgetary support to these activities. These latter measures, even without any substantial reorganization, would make a mighty difference.

Strengthening existing agencies

A third and more immediately urgent requirement of strategy is a general strengthening of all main existing organizations active in this field, public and private. This requires especially an upgrading of personnel and of the status of these activities. One heartening recent event was the appointment of a distinguished American scholar on Japan to head the USIS in Tokyo, with the provision that he would devote his attention especially to educational and cultural affairs, leaving main responsibility for information activities to a well qualified deputy.

The Office of Education is notoriously in need of upgrading. With the United States Commissioner of Education ranking third level from the top in his own and other Departments—roughly equivalent to an Assistant Secretary of Agriculture in the federal pecking order—it is difficult to see how the man somewhere below him with prime concern for the international aspects of American education is going to carry sufficient weight in the Washington bureaucracy to make the Office of Education as strong a force as it should be in this field.

So long as cultural affairs in our embassies are substantially outranked by top economic and military officers, and work below the Public Affairs Officer (whose first concern is usually current information), it is hard to see how these posts will attract enough outstanding people or how the United States will be adequately represented abroad in the educational and cultural field.

And so long as the Bureau of Educational and Cultural Affairs of the State Department—which manages a business as large and at least as complex as a good-sized department store—does not have a single super-grade position, a good recruiting service, or reasonable freedom of action on personnel, it is difficult to see how the Bureau's programs can be managed with satisfactory efficiency or effectiveness.

No single factor is more important to the success of educational and cultural programs than the quality and competence of the people who run them. This is truer of these activities than of many other types in which the government engages. We have been blessed far beyond what we deserve in the ability and dedication of the people in government and in major private organizations who have functioned in this field. But we cannot stretch our luck further. If the national effort is to be expanded, stronger administration will be required. These programs can no longer be operated on an administrative shoestring. We must pay for quality performance and will save much money in the end by doing so.

*   *   *

This, in brief, is where we have been, where we are, some of the needs and opportunities that face us in the future, and some of the measures required to meet them.

What stands out above all else is, first, that educational, scientific and cultural affairs must play an essential role in our relations with the world if our most fundamental national and human goals are to be achieved and, second, that in this area of foreign relations more than in any other, the national effort must be national in the fullest sense.

It is abundantly clear that the United States has great resources of talent and institutions to bring to bear in this area of foreign policy and that it would be decidedly in keeping with our national tradition and our national interest to apply them more fully. It is, after all, our traditional devotion to educational opportunity for all, our dedication to the idea that every individual, regardless of the circumstances of his birth, should have a chance to rise to his full potential—far more than our gadgets, our financial wealth and our military might—that has won worldwide respect for our society. We would be foolish indeed to neglect the full use of this great asset as we struggle toward the goal of a peaceful world in which all people can enjoy similar freedom and opportunity. If there is a road to peace it surely lies in this direction.

Final Report of the Twenty-second American Assembly

At the close of their discussions the participants in the Twenty-second American Assembly at Arden House, Harriman, New York, October 18-21, 1962, on CULTURAL AFFAIRS AND FOREIGN RELATIONS, reviewed as a group the following statement. Although there was general agreement on the Final Report, it is not the practice of The American Assembly for participants to affix their signatures, and it should not be assumed that every participant necessarily subscribes to every recommendation.

Introduction

Cultural affairs comprise the broad realm of educational, intellectual, scientific, and artistic activity. They are an essential and integral part of international relations, for they are concerned with contacts between people, the exchange of ideas, and the expression and confrontation of cultural and social ideals.

The great and growing importance of international cultural affairs derives from the vast increase in communications, the prominence of the United States in world affairs, and new ambitions for economic and social development throughout the world. The competition with the communist countries as well as the emergence of many new nations add political dimensions.

The government and the public need to recognize more than at present that cultural activities serve the long-term objectives and ideals of the United States. They enrich the life of mankind, help establish the international climate in which we live, nourish our national life and reflect both the ideals and frustrations of the people of the world. They increase the understanding and appreciation of other cultures in this country. They are of immense significance. Their political impact is also considerable, for they can contribute to the building of stable and progressive societies and affect the prestige and influence of the United States abroad.

Cultural activities also serve our broader goals by giving expression to individual talents and national ideals. Attempts to make them attain quick political results are usually self-defeating and futile.

The character of our society leaves with private initiative major responsibility for international cultural activity. Historically, private individuals and organizations have been effective pioneers in the field. Today, their responsibilities and undertakings are increasing faster than the resources to support them, and there is need for greater governmental effort. Such effort should, however, supplement and encourage private endeavor. Governmental support of private effort should be increased without adversely affecting the private character of these programs and their effectiveness.

Private activities take place in an infinite variety of ways. They have an enormous, though not sharply defined, capacity to serve the United States in international understanding, either well or poorly. Alongside the broad program of the philanthropic foundations are the more specialized but often extensive activities of learned societies and religious, labor, fraternal, and other organizations. There are also the frequently haphazard but often successful efforts of individuals and communities. The American serviceman and tourist abroad, the teacher of a foreign student, the writer with a foreign audience all make their contribution to international cultural relations. Deep cultural influences also result from commercial activities—the news agencies, motion pictures, radio and television, and the many companies with overseas operations.

The quality and vitality of our educational and intellectual life at home are indispensable foundations for influence abroad. Our cultural activities reflect the state of our national culture. American international cultural activity must grow out of an effective implementation of democratic ideals at home. We should attempt to portray our ideals and aspirations but never seek to project an image of America that does not correspond to reality. We must continue to learn from others and adapt our knowledge and outlook to a world of spectacular change. Parochialism would be stultifying to our ideals and disastrous for our policies.

Our society is rooted in the Western heritage; our cultural ties with the West have been continuous, but require constant strengthening. However, ties need to be strengthened with countries whose traditions and social structures are largely unfamiliar to us. In dealing with all nations the cultural relationship should be reciprocal.

The United States is eminently qualified to carry on international scientific and technological programs. The sciences, both natural and social, offer a valuable bridge toward understanding between ourselves and other intellectual communities. The sciences provide a vehicle for contact even with the communist countries, since they respect our achievements in this field. In the less developed countries, well-designed scientific programs can contribute substantially to national development, to the training of local scientists and to our own knowledge.

Cultural exchanges also make it possible for artists and members of the intellectual community generally to communicate across national boundaries as creative individuals. Such exchanges enlarge appreciation of the cultural resources of other countries. It is essential in these exchanges to respect the integrity and freedom of the artist and scholar which are indispensable to his creativity. Such exchanges also permit the expression of intellectual and artistic ideals even across the barriers of the Cold War.

Education is heavily involved in international affairs because of its close relation to international understanding. In other countries—particularly those that are newly developing—there is a fervent desire for educational advancement and a deep interest in the unique characteristics of American education.

The United States needs further to define its cultural relations with the communist countries where cultural activities, international as well as domestic, are instruments of national policy subject to complete governmental control. Exchanges with these countries can become a snare for the unwary and a delusion for the uninformed. Nevertheless, cultural relations may be one of the few means whereby better understanding can be encouraged and perilous tensions reduced. In any event, we must not close our doors or narrowly confine our exchanges, thus falling into the trap of imitating our adversaries.

In view of the significance of international cultural affairs and in the desire to encourage sound policies and arrangements for their guidance and execution, this American Assembly makes the following recommendations.

RECOMMENDATIONS

1. Every effort should be made to increase public awareness of the importance of international cultural activities to the pursuit of America's ideals as a nation and to the realization of its national purposes.

2. Cultural activities should not be confused with or subordinated to information and propaganda programs. Nor should they be expected to serve short-term, political ends, but conducted rather with the expectation of long-term results.

3. The American public can and should give more generous support to the government's international cultural activities. At the same time, within the broad framework of American foreign policy, the government

should offer encouragement and assistance to private activities without imposing political restraints on them.

Cooperation between the government and the private sector has been effectively achieved in the Fulbright and other programs. Such common endeavors should be expanded and extended to other areas so that the fullest use may be made of all resources in the execution of international cultural activities.

4. There should be an improvement and increase in private American participation in international cultural activity by foundations and educational institutions as well as business, labor, civic, religious and professional organizations, including many that are not now active in this field. Private efforts, like those of government, must be carefully planned and based on an adequate understanding of the situations with which they deal.

5. American international cultural activity should build a firm base in this country for the understanding of foreign cultures through our schools, universities, communities and mass media. International exchange programs can and should be used more extensively to increase our understanding and to enrich our own society.

6. We should respond as effectively and as generously as we can to the needs of the newly emerging countries for assistance in those educational, scientific and other cultural fields where our experience and other resources can help them.

We should seek the further cooperation of like-minded nations and agencies in this vast undertaking.

To achieve these ends greater financial resources and improved institutional arrangements are needed.

7. The United States should participate vigorously in the educational development of the emerging nations. This entails satisfactory arrangements for the selection, placement and follow-up of students and other visitors who come to this country. It requires an understanding of the needs in each country and our willingness and ability to provide advisors, teachers, teaching aids and research on the application of modern educational techniques to local needs. It should also involve specific efforts to strengthen international communication and cooperation in research. In this way the scholars of these countries will come into increasingly close association with the world intellectual community and bring the contributions of their fields to bear more effectively in the development of their countries.

8. We should maintain and strengthen our cultural exchanges with those countries of the West with which we share a common heritage and whose present and future are intimately bound up with ours.

9. Cultural exchanges with the Soviet Union and communist countries of Eastern Europe should be expanded. These exchanges should be pursued independently of short-term fluctuations in Cold War relation-

ships and should not necessarily be contingent on precise matching arrangements.

10. The possibility should not be excluded of establishing cultural contact, perhaps through private channels, with the people of Communist China under conditions that would ensure useful exchanges.

11. Cultural activities, whether carried out by government or private effort, should be carefully adapted to the needs of each area and country. Standardized programs should be avoided and care and sensitivity to local needs and interests should be exercised at all times.

12. Cultural exchanges should have the further advice and participation of the best representatives of American creative talent.

13. The significance of the sciences as ingredients of cultural programs needs to be more adequately recognized. Policies to guide and strengthen the government's international scientific activity should be developed, and effective ways devised to get the maximum benefit from international scientific communication and activity.

14. Commercial enterprises should appreciate and give continuing consideration to the international impact of their activities and cultural products.

The impact abroad of some films, TV programs and other mass media now being exported tends to negate the favorable effects of our other efforts in international cultural activities. Efforts should be made and, if necessary, financial assistance provided to assure wider distribution abroad of high quality radio and television programs and films.

15. Government and private organizations should further facilitate the distribution of American publications abroad, both in the original and in translation, through the encouragement and expansion of programs such as The Information Media Guaranty and Franklin Publications and through the strengthening of American libraries abroad. The Information Media Guaranty programs should be authorized to include the entire range of American creative talent and scholarship. Translations into English of more good foreign books should also be encouraged.

16. In view of weaknesses in the present organization of governmental administrative machinery in the field of cultural relations, immediate action is urged to bring an early correction of continuing hindrances to effective governmental cultural activity.

17. The need for outstanding career officers in the cultural field should be recognized, and encouragement given to the long-term training of foreign service officers in cultural affairs and of cultural officers in foreign affairs. Service in cultural affairs should be recognized as equally important with service in other branches of foreign affairs.

18. The proposed career officers in cultural affairs should be supplemented by leaders from scholarly, artistic, and scientific communities who would serve abroad for limited periods and be free of routine administrative work.

19. Cultural affairs can often be pursued effectively through multilateral organizations, and full advantage should be taken of these opportunities. In particular, the United States should participate more vigorously in the affairs of UNESCO.

20. The Fulbright-Hays Act makes possible an expanded and improved United States cultural program. Congress and the Executive Branch of the government are urged to provide the necessary funds.

Participants in the Twenty-second American Assembly

MILDRED ADAMS
New York City

GEORGE V. ALLEN
President
The Tobacco Institute
Washington, D. C.

JAMES F. BARIE
Bureau of the Budget
Washington, D. C.

LUCIUS BATTLE
Assistant Secretary of State
  for Educational and Cultural
  Affairs
Washington, D. C.

WILLIAM BENTON
Publisher
Encyclopaedia Britannica
New York

ROBERT BLUM
Council on Foreign Relations
New York

PAUL J. BRAISTED
President
The Hazen Foundation
New Haven

WALLACE R. BRODE
Washington, D. C.

JOHN J. BROOKS
President
International Schools Foundation
New York

JOHN ANTHONY BROWN
Vice President
Occidental College
California

STEPHEN GOFF BROWN
Harriman Scholar
Columbia University

FREDERICK BURKHARDT
President
American Council of Learned
  Societies
New York

CASS CANFIELD
Chairman
Harper & Row
New York

GORDON R. CLAPP
President
Development and Resources Corp.
New York

JOHN D. CONNORS
A.F.L.-C.I.O.
Washington, D. C.

DONALD COOK
Director
Educational & Cultural Exchange
Department of State
Washington, D. C.

PHILIP H. COOMBS
The Brookings Institution
Washington, D. C.

LOUIS G. COWAN
Director
Communications Research Center
Brandeis University
Massachusetts

ROBERT CRAIG
Executive Director
Aspen Institute for Humanistic Studies
Colorado

KEVIN FREDERICK
CUNNINGHAM
Harriman Scholar
Columbia University

WILLIAM DIX
University Library
Princeton University

JOHN W. F. DULLES
University of Texas

VERNON A. EAGLE
Executive Director
New World Foundation
New York

C. J. ELIEZER
Deputy Vice Chancellor
University of Malaya
Kuala Lumpur

HERBERT E. EVANS
President
People's Broadcasting Corporation
Columbus

JOHN R. EVERETT
President
Britannica Press
Chicago

JULIAN B. FEIBELMAN
Rabbi
Temple Sinai
New Orleans

JULIUS FLEISCHMANN
Chairman
Fleischmann Foundation
Cincinnati

LUTHER H. FOSTER
President
Tuskegee Institute
Alabama

LLOYD A. FREE
Director
Institute of International Social
Research
Princeton, New Jersey

JOHN GARDNER
President
Carnegie Corporation
New York

ROSAMOND GILDER
U. S. Director
International Theatre Institute
New York

AUGUST HECKSCHER
Special White House
Consultant on the Arts
Washington, D. C.

HARRY GOLDBERG
A.F.L.-C.I.O.
Washington, D. C.

RICHARD H. HEINDEL
President
Pratt Institute
Brooklyn

LOY W. HENDERSON
The American University
Washington, D. C.

GERTRUDE S. HOOKER
The Ford Foundation
New York

HAROLD B. HOSKINS
Millbrook, N. Y.

JOSEPH D. HUGHES
Richard King Mellon Foundation
Pittsburgh

PHILIP E. JACOB
University of Pennsylvania

JOSEPH M. JONES
Washington, D. C.

WALTER H. C. LAVES
Chairman
Department of Government
University of Indiana

COL. G. A. LINCOLN
Head, Department of Social Studies
United States Military Academy
West Point

W. McNEIL LOWRY
The Ford Foundation
New York

DAVID W. MacEACHRON
Council on Foreign Relations
New York

JAMES JOHN MANDROS
Harriman Scholar
Columbia University

MRS. MAURICE T. MOORE, III
Chairman
Institute of International Education
New York

WALDEMAR NIELSEN
President
African-American Institute
New York

CHESTER W. NIMITZ, Jr.
Vice President
Perkin-Elmer Corporation
Norwalk, Connecticut

ROGER REVELLE
Science Advisor to the
  Secretary of the Interior
Washington, D. C.

HILLYARD RODERICK
Division of Research
Atomic Energy Commission
Washington, D. C.

MERRITT KIRK RUDDOCK
Belvedere, California

C. V. R. SCHUYLER
General, U.S.A. (Ret.)
Office of the Governor
Albany

ROBERT SHEEKS
The Asia Foundation
San Francisco

ALBERT G. SIMS
Executive Vice President
Institute of International Education
New York

LAUREN K. SOTH
Editor of the Editorial Page
Des Moines *Register & Tribune*
Iowa

WILLIAM E. SPAULDING
President
Houghton, Mifflin Company
Boston

ROBERT H. THAYER
Associate Director
American Field Service
New York

KENNETH W. THOMPSON
Vice President
The Rockefeller Foundation
New York

M. H. TRYTTEN
Director
Office of Scientific Personnel
National Academy of Sciences
Washington, D. C.

GERRITT VANDER ENDE
President
Pacific First Federal Savings
  and Loan Association
Tacoma

KOERT S. VOORHEES
President
Polygon Corporation
Cedar Falls, Iowa

HOWARD E. WILSON
Dean
School of Education
U.C.L.A.

PEGGY WOOD
New York

BARBARA WRISTON
Director
Museum Education
The Art Institute of Chicago

PHILIP YOUNG
Executive Director
U. S. Council of International
    Chamber of Commerce
New York

The American Assembly

Since its establishment by Dwight D. Eisenhower at Columbia University in 1950, The American Assembly has held Assemblies of national leaders and has published books to illuminate issues of United States policy.

The Assembly is a national, nonpartisan educational institution, incorporated under the State of New York. It was the official administrator of the President's

Commission on National Goals, which reported to President Eisenhower late in 1960.

The Trustees of the Assembly approve a topic for presentation in a background book, authoritatively designed and written to aid deliberations at national Assembly sessions at Arden House, the Harriman Campus of Columbia University. These books are also used to support discussion at regional Assembly sessions and to evoke consideration by the general public.

All sessions of the Assembly, whether international, national or local, issue and publicize independent reports of conclusions and recommendations on the topic at hand. Participants in these sessions constitute a wide range of experience and competence. The following institutions have cooperated or are scheduled to cooperate with the Assembly in sponsoring sessions across the country and abroad.

University of Arizona
University of Arkansas
The Associated Colleges of the Midwest
Aspen Institute
Battelle Memorial Institute
Brigham Young University
Brown University
University of California (Berkeley)
University of California (Los Angeles)
Cleveland Council on World Affairs
University of Colorado
Creighton University
Dallas Council on World Affairs
University of Denver
Drake University
Duke University
Emory University
University of Florida
Foreign Policy Assoc. of Pittsburgh
University of Illinois
Indiana University
State University of Iowa
The Institute for Strategic Studies (London)
The Johnson Foundation
Kansas City International Relations Council
Lawrence College
Michigan State University
University of Minnesota

Minnesota World Affairs Center
University of Missouri
University of Nebraska
University of New Mexico
North Central Association of Colleges and Secondary Schools
Occidental College
University of Oklahoma
University of Oregon
The Principia College
University of Puerto Rico
William Marsh Rice University
Ripon College
Southern Methodist University
Southwestern at Memphis
Stanford University
St. Louis University
Town Hall of Los Angeles
University of Texas
Tufts University
Tulane University
United States Air Force Academy
Vanderbilt University
University of Vermont
University of Washington
Washington University
Western Reserve University
University of Wisconsin
World Affairs Council of Northern California
University of Wyoming

American Assembly books are purchased and put to use by thousands of individuals, libraries, businesses, public agencies, non-governmental organizations, educational institutions, discussion meetings and service groups. The following are completed, continuing or future subjects of study by the American Assembly.

1963—THE UNITED STATES AND LATIN AMERICA (SECOND EDITION)
    —THE POPULATION DILEMMA (JULY)
1962—AUTOMATION AND TECHNOLOGICAL CHANGE
    —CULTURAL AFFAIRS AND FOREIGN RELATIONS
    —THE UNITED STATES AND THE FAR EAST (SECOND EDITION)

1961—ARMS CONTROL
    —OUTER SPACE

1960—THE SECRETARY OF STATE
    —THE FEDERAL GOVERNMENT AND HIGHER EDUCATION

    Library, cloth bound edition, $3.95
    Spectrum, paper bound edition, $1.95
    Available from better booksellers and Prentice-Hall, Inc.

———————————

The following titles were published by The American Assembly. Prices indicate books which can be obtained by writing to The American Assembly.

1959—THE UNITED STATES AND LATIN AMERICA (FIRST EDITION)
    —WAGES, PRICES, PROFITS AND PRODUCTIVITY ($2.00)

1958—THE UNITED STATES AND AFRICA (FIRST EDITION)
    —UNITED STATES MONETARY POLICY ($2.00)

1957—ATOMS FOR POWER ($1.00)
    —INTERNATIONAL STABILITY AND PROGRESS

1956—THE UNITED STATES AND THE FAR EAST (FIRST EDITION)
    —THE REPRESENTATION OF THE UNITED STATES ABROAD

1955—THE FORTY-EIGHT STATES
    —UNITED STATES AGRICULTURE

1954—THE FEDERAL GOVERNMENT SERVICE
    —THE UNITED STATES STAKE IN THE UNITED NATIONS

1953—ECONOMIC SECURITY FOR AMERICANS

1952—INFLATION

1951—UNITED STATES-WESTERN EUROPE RELATIONSHIPS

Regular readers of The American Assembly receive early copies of each new Assembly study and are billed subsequently. To enroll as a regular reader please write:

Prentice-Hall, Inc., Englewood Cliffs, N.J.